QUOTATIONS
FROM THE PUBLIC COMMENTS OF

ARSÈNE WENGER

MANAGER, ARSENAL FOOTBALL CLUB

QUOTATIONS
FROM THE PUBLIC COMMENTS OF

ARSÈNE WENGER

MANAGER, ARSENAL FOOTBALL CLUB

Compiled by DAVID MANSON

First published in Great Britain in 2005 by
Virgin Books
Thames Wharf Studios
Rainville Road
London W6 9HA

A catalogue record for the book is available from
the British Library.

ISBN 978-0-7535-3907-1

Typeset by Phoenix Photosetting, Chatham, Kent

Penguin Random House is committed to a sustainable future for
our business, our readers and our planet. This book is made from
Forest Stewardship Council® certified paper.

MIX
Paper | Supporting
responsible forestry
FSC® C018179
www.fsc.org

Printed and bound in Great Britain by Clays Ltd, St Ives plc

CONTENTS

ACKNOWLEDGEMENTS

I offer my grateful thanks to all those mentioned in the Sources at the end of this book, whose earlier efforts have greatly facilitated my own task in preparing this work. In addition, from a personal point of view, I would like to thank my mother and my brothers, along with Dave, Charlotte and little Lexine, Rob H, Dave B, John B, Phil S at the *Stratford Journal* and all at arsenal-mania.com for their support in this project.

In conclusion, and as a lifelong Arsenal supporter, I offer my deepest gratitude to Arsène Wenger himself for his achievements to date. Like all other Arsenal fans, I can only hope that the years documented within these pages are, indeed, only the beginning ...

David Manson
March 2005

Genesis

In August 1996, very few Arsenal fans had heard of Arsène Wenger. When the 1996–97 season began, Bruce Rioch was team manager at Highbury, and apparently he was secure in his job. But just six weeks into the new season, Rioch had been sacked and replaced by a Frenchman known to almost no Englishman, with the notable exception of Arsenal vice-chairman David Dein.

Arsène Wenger joined Arsenal from the Japanese club Grampus Eight, where he had gone to work after a successful seven years in charge of Monaco. But it was still a largely unknown figure who arrived at Highbury to give his first press conference on Sunday, 22 September 1996. That morning, a slim, studious-looking 46-year-old introduced himself to the awaiting press, and a new chapter in the story of Arsenal Football Club began.

At that first press conference, it became obvious that the urbane, university-educated Wenger would bring a new way of thinking to the cliché-ridden world of English football. But, with hindsight, one can see that, in his early public comments, he set his stall out early doors.

'I had the feeling the club needed me, and I wanted to be here.'

'If I'm here it's not because I'm a friend of the vice-chairman of Arsenal. It's because the board of Arsenal think I have the right qualities to work here, and it's up to me to prove they made the right choice.'

'I love English football because the roots of football are here. I like the spirit of the games, and at Arsenal I like the appearance of the club and the potential of the club.'

'I want to improve the squad with my ideas.'

'My message to the fans is come here and watch us and be happy.'

22 September 1996 – Introductory comments on a Sunday morning in North London.

'I tried to watch the Spurs match on television in my hotel yesterday, but I fell asleep.'

23 September 1996 – and already endearing himself to Arsenal supporters.

'My challenge is to mix the English style to a more continental way. Also I am conscious that I have to win over the supporters because they don't really know me and I am foreign. But if they reject me it will not be because I am foreign. They will reject me if I don't do a good job.'

25 September 1996 – well aware that his appointment was greeted by many Arsenal fans with a sense of bafflement. Some of these fans were perfectly happy for an overseas coach to replace Bruce Rioch when they thought it would be Johan Cruyff, and not Arsène Who?

'Without doubt I am going to look in France [for new Arsenal players].'

11 October 1996 – a statement of intent.

'I know that for the confidence of the team and for my future works it would be important to start with a victory . . . if I'd started with a loss everyone would have spoken about it.'

12 October 1996 – after his first game in charge against Blackburn results in a 2–0 win for Arsenal. Both goals were scored by Ian Wright, and Patrick Vieira was the only non-Briton in the Arsenal side.

'Foreigners are bringing bad things as well as good things to the game here.'

21 December 1996 – after Nottingham Forest's Croatian player Nikola Jerkan reacts theatrically to contact with Ian Wright, and the Arsenal player is sent off.

'I would never accept second place as enough but in terms of European football it is really just the same and all we can do is try to finish as high as possible.'

14 March 1997 – Arsenal have a chance of winning the Premiership, just five months after Wenger takes over. And, with Champions League football no longer restricted to League champions, the runners-up spot is worthy of pursuit in its own right.

'Although I never thought we could be champions [in 1996–97] when I arrived at Arsenal we are now in a good position among six teams who could win it: Manchester, Newcastle, Wimbledon, Liverpool, Chelsea and ourselves.'

19 March 1997 – and still Wenger thinks of winning the title in a close-run race which did indeed involve Wimbledon.

'The race is now for the second place and, fortunately, second place may be as important as first, really.'

19 April 1997 – Arsenal concede an unfortunate late goal to Blackburn, leading to an equally unfortunate third-place Premiership finish behind Newcastle and champions Manchester United.

> 'It is strange that Manchester United should be complaining like this because it becomes a bigger problem when you allow it to dominate your thinking.'

11 April 1997 – a taste of things to come! Manchester United's successes in 1996–97 had created a situation where they would have to play their last four Premiership games in an eight-day period. The club moaned about this, but to no avail, after Arsène Wenger (and others) had expressed opposition to extending the season for United's benefit. At this point, United manager Alex Ferguson launched an extraordinary attack on his Arsenal counterpart, which is worth quoting in full. 'He has no experience of English football. He's come from Japan. And now he's into English football and he is now telling everybody in England how to organise their football. I think he should keep his mouth shut. Firmly shut.' Unfortunately for Scotsman Ferguson, Arsène Wenger would keep his mouth very much open, according to circumstances, in the years ahead.

Monsieur

When Arsène Wenger came to Arsenal in 1996, he was a Frenchman. Nine years later, he still was. But in 2005, there was nothing unusual about overseas managers working at the top of English football, both at club and international level. It was a different story when Monsieur Wenger first arrived at Highbury.

When appointed, Wenger became only the second-ever foreign coach to manage a top English club having played no football in England himself, and the earlier reign of Josef Venglos at Aston Villa had been a total failure. But Arsène Wenger would enjoy huge success in England as he set about imposing his deeply-held beliefs on football and footballers, both on and off the field.

From the beginning, Wenger set out to transform the famously laddish lifestyles then practised by players at many English clubs, Arsenal included. By chance, just prior to Wenger's arrival, Tony Adams had decided to abandon his own boozing ways, and so it was a sober Arsenal captain who led an increasingly fit team of Arsenal footballers, with every aspect of their diet, fitness and training monitored by Wenger and his technical staff.

This was all new in the English game, but even as Wenger set about changing old English attitudes, his public comments revealed a man deeply in love with English football, a game to which his own contribution would be fully recognised.

'To go to another country with a football club at a high level and be successful is a big challenge for me.'

22 September 1996 – Wenger looks forward to the years ahead.

'There was only one previous example of offering such a job to a person like me, who had never played in England, a country with over a century of football history. That's only natural. With a history like that, it was almost unthinkable to turn to an outsider for help. It was like Japan turning to France for a sumo manager.'

Later reflections on the near-unique circumstances of his appointment as Arsenal manager.

'The English train less than the French. For them [the English], as long as they have given their all in a match, training is just an accessory. I am trying to change that attitude, to make them realise that training is crucial.'

Getting down to work, late in 1996 ...

'I like players to relax with massages and hot baths. I
believe they are helpful, physically and psychologically.'

... having made the decision to employ a dedicated masseur.

'I think in England you eat too much sugar and meat and
not enough vegetables.'

18 October 1996.

'You can't survive today at the top level ... if you don't
have a healthy life.'

25 March 1999.

'When cards [are] played for nearly nothing it is great. But
when the purpose is big money you have to forbid it
because it spoils your mind.'

**6 November 2000 – no big-money card games on the Arsenal
team coach.**

'To play at the top level you have to have control over your life and part of that is to do with mental strength.'

8 March 2004 – Wenger finally bans Arsenal players from drinking alcohol at all, having long since closed down the once-famous players' bar.

'Everyone has a private life and so do I … I have a girlfriend in the South of France. I have lived with her for three years, but that is my business.'

9 November 1996 – girlfriend Annie and their daughter Léa would later join Arsène Wenger at his home in England, but without formally marrying.

'I am in a bad position to say it because I'm not married, but I'm happy if my players are married or in a stable relationship. They are the same players but they are better mentally, have better discipline and more emotional stability. If you have to go out every night to find a girl when you are 21 or 22 it's not the best way to prepare for a football game.'

10 April 1999 – questioning the value of a laddish social life for footballers.

'I watch football ... one of the good things about being in England is that most matches are played on a Sunday. I watch games on most days and I have a large library of video tapes.'

May 1999 – Wenger reveals how he chooses to spend his leisure time.

'I don't go out. I have a lot of interest in theatre and movies and when I wasn't a manager I watched a lot. Now I just don't have the time.'

25 January 2002.

'I don't have a life outside football. When people ask me how I like London, I say, "Where is London?"'

28 September 2002 – Wenger reveals the all-consuming nature of his work with Arsenal.

'Fair play is an English word. It is not a French word, and it has been copied all over the world. Unfortunately, it does not function any more here.'

19 April 1997 – showing his early knowledge of English culture, after a breach of the throw-in-after-injury etiquette by Blackburn's Chris Sutton leads to a goal that costs Arsenal a place in the Champions League. Years later, Sutton's act still rankled with Wenger, who would respond famously to a similar *faux pas* by one of his own players.

'In England, football is important for everybody.'

22 November 1996.

'By 2006 it will be forty years since England last staged the World Cup finals. I think that after that amount of time it should return to the country where football was created.'

13 February 1997 – a Frenchman cheers on England's ill-fated bid to host football's biggest tournament.

'If I can help Arsenal and England I'll do it. But I'm not responsible for England.'

20 April 1998 – on the subject of an injured Ian Wright, whose chances of playing in the 1998 World Cup were threatened by his lack of first-team football at Arsenal.

'It is too easy to say England went out of the World Cup because of David Beckham.'

9 August 1998 – Wenger has his say on the Manchester United player who had endured a summer of media hatred. This followed a World Cup second-round game in which Beckham was sent off for petulantly kicking Argentina's Diego Simeone. Beckham was blamed for England's subsequent exit from the tournament by England manager Glenn Hoddle and, most venomously of all, the English tabloid press.

'Beckham is not a dirty player. Only in World Cups.'

20 September 1998 – Wenger in jovial mood after Arsenal secure an emphatic win over Manchester United, David Beckham and all.

'I work in this country [England] and I am always telling people how good the game is here.'

22 July 2000.

'I am not as pessimistic as many people in England. I personally believe there are very good players in England.'

13 October 2000 – Wenger refuses to share English gloom following the national team's dismal start to the World Cup qualifiers, and the resignation of Kevin Keegan as manager ...

'Maybe England can win it. OK, you lost at home to Germany, but maybe you'll win in Germany.'

... and reflecting on England's World Cup-qualifying defeat at Wembley. So poor a performance was this that few within English football thought it possible that England could win the 2001 return fixture in Germany. Wenger was one of them. Less than a year later, under Sven-Göran Eriksson, England won 5–1 in Munich.

'That job is not for me.'

24 October 2000 – Wenger ruling himself out of the England reckoning ...

'My mind is not like the English weather forecast. It does not constantly change.'

... and confirming his disinterest in the England manager's job, again ...

'I have not heard [Sven-Göran] Eriksson say that he does not want the job.'

... but suggesting another possible candidate to fill the vacancy.

'I think the championship in England is more difficult than anywhere else, maybe. The commitment is higher than anywhere else in the world. Listen, last night I had the choice between Cannes and Nantes on French TV and Middlesbrough against Manchester City in Division One. And after half an hour I switched to Middlesbrough–Manchester City. Because there was more passion around the field.'

18 April 1998 – on viewing choices during a night in at home.

'It's difficult to know how people see me ... I feel more a manager who loves football than specifically that I come from a different country. I'm the same nationality as everybody who loves football.'

1 May 1998.

'They [Kanu and Diawara] need to get used to this kind of fight, and that was good practice for them today. Welcome to English football.'

3 April 1999 – after a hard-fought, highly physical goalless draw with Southampton, the kind of game with which Arsenal's recently signed African players were still largely unfamiliar.

'Sometimes now, when I watch continental games on television, I'm a bit bored. I ask, "Where is the intensity?"'

2 August 1999.

'We need not just quality in our passing and calmness, but power. English power.'

4 April 2001 – pleading for Anglo-Saxon potency in a forthcoming Champions League encounter with Valencia.

'I don't kick dressing-room doors, or the cat, or even journalists.'

23 November 2001 – outlining his management style to the press, and perhaps offering a contrast with more 'traditional' football managers within the English game.

'For the time being, England is the best place to work in world football. I want to continue here for as long as it pleases me and as long as people are happy with me.'

12 January 2001 – talking up *l'Angleterre* to the media in his native country in an interview translated by the English media from the French, one of five languages spoken fluently by Arsène Wenger.

'It is a great honour to be given this individual award but, as football is a team sport, I must give a great deal of credit and recognition to everyone that has helped me since I became manager of Arsenal in 1996.'

12 June 2003 – on the news of his honorary OBE.

Gunners 1

In August 1996, the Arsenal team featured only one overseas player, the prodigiously gifted Dutchman Dennis Bergkamp, who joined the club under the Bruce Rioch regime. The rest of the team were doughty Britons, with the star player undoubtedly Ian Wright, a striker of traditionally English goalscoring virtues.

But, even before Rioch's successor took over, things began to change at Arsenal. By the time Arsène Wenger gave his first press conference, the twenty-year-old Frenchman Patrick Vieira had agreed to join the club. By the start of the 1997–98 season, he had been joined by fellow countrymen Nicolas Anelka and Emmanuel Petit, as well as Bergkamp's compatriot Marc Overmars, all of whose talents were fully appreciated by their new club manager.

The overseas arrivals did bring a new sophistication to Arsenal's football and, as the seasons passed, Wenger's teams have become ever more international in composition. But, during Wenger's early years, one part of his team remained wholly home grown. In the early 1990s, the then Arsenal boss George Graham built the best defence in England. As Wenger took over, this defensive unit remained intact and the new manager saw no reason for change.

'If you project ten years into the future, the best teams in England will play with seven or eight foreign players.'

Late 1996 – early prophecies of what is to come.

'If you bring players in, you have to make sure they have the right spirit, because it's important not to destroy your spirit.'

16 November 1996.

'I have a deep respect for my squad.'

23 November 1996 – prior to Wenger's first derby game against Spurs.

'He's a celebration specialist.'

24 November 1996 – after Wenger's first victorious derby game against Spurs, during which Ian Wright removed his shirt after scoring to reveal a vest sporting the message 'I love the lads'.

'He [Ian Wright] can have one TV show, if it doesn't take up too much time.'

10 January 1998 – when questioned about Wright's showbiz ambitions.

'When Ian Wright is going well you must put him in jail to keep him out of the game.'

28 March 1998 – when Ian Wright was still a footballer.

'[Martin Keown's] movie career is probably over.'

10 April 1998 – and still with showbiz in response to Arsenal's defender requiring stitches to a facial injury sustained in the FA Cup semi-final against Wolves. Few were aware that Keown's movie career had ever begun.

'Davor Suker is the type of player we have needed.'

10 September 1999 – on signing the well-known Croatian striker.

'We will be letting him [Suker] go.'

14 April 2000 – but not for that long.

'[Vieira is] a great midfielder because he's a fighter.'

22 September 1996 – on signing the then little-known Patrick Vieira.

'He [Vieira] has everything you want from a midfielder.'

17 February 1999 – one satisfied manager.

'We want him [Vieira] to be forever at Arsenal.'

16 August 2000 – expressing sentiments shared by many Arsenal supporters on the subject of Patrick Vieira.

'Vieira was a giant from the first to the last minute.'

21 September 2000 – praise for Vieira after a towering performance at West Ham, a year on from a game at Upton Park when Vieira's performance had been all too human.

'I can show you Patrick's shin protector. It's broken and full of blood.'

6 January 2001 – after Vieira is the victim of an horrific tackle in an FA Cup tie at Carlisle. This was a far from unprecedented incident, and Wenger was pleased that, on this occasion, his player did not react to the foul play against him.

'He's not always the devil people think he is. He's gone nineteen games now without a booking – it's a long time, too long, he's too soft!'

11 January 2001 – an ironic response to a relatively peaceful period of Patrick Vieira's Arsenal career.

'We need a big squad. But it's always a very fine line to keep everyone happy and have good players when you need [them]. That could be about twenty players. If you go to 25 or 30 players, and they never play, you lose what makes you strong.'

25 April 1998.

'My team is only two years of age.'

27 February 1999 – Wenger's Double-winning side appears to be still in its infancy!

'I think after every match he comes in with a bottle of champagne. He can open a shop now.'

19 January 1997 – on another man-of-the-match performance by Dennis Bergkamp.

'He's 27 … at his age you can become a huge player or go backwards.'

Directing Bergkamp to the career crossroads at the end of the 1996–97 season.

'Dennis is a playmaker and a striker … you feel he always knows which position is the biggest threat to his opponent. Sometimes it's up front, sometimes he's in between the lines, sometimes he's in midfield.'

24 September 1997 – on Bergkamp's uncanny gifts.

'There was too much holding of Dennis Bergkamp. We must buy him an extra shirt.'

16 February 1998 – after a goalless draw with Crystal Palace, Wenger ponders a sartorial solution to opposition defenders grabbing hold of Arsenal's superstar.

'He's like a Formula One car – everything has to be in order.'

15 May 1998 – more on Bergkamp, the wholly engineered footballer.

'He [Bergkamp] is very influential because he can pass, finish and give the final ball. When he is not there we look less dangerous because that final ball doesn't come.'

6 February 1999.

'Dennis is like a pianist who works at his skill.'

19 February 1999 – and yet further thoughts on the arts of Bergkamp ...

'When you have Bergkamp behind you, you know you will get the ball.'

... who still called the tune when the Arsenal team moved forwards.

'We wanted to get in winner-types because of the specific Arsenal spirit, which is a winner-type who will never give up. Emmanuel and Marc are these type of players.'

22 June 1997 – announcing the signing of Marc Overmars and Emmanuel Petit for fees of £7,000,000 and £2,500,000 respectively ...

'Marc Overmars is a player of class.'

... and Arsenal fans begin to suspect that times are changing.

'Emmanuel [Petit] will never be an easy player to manage ... he's an intelligent player who won't put up with mediocrity ... he'll never be happy with just picking up his money.'

3 January 1999.

'I was told Nicolas [Anelka] was unhappy. He wanted to leave Paris … maybe because I was French he came and became one of our players.'

September 1998 – words to Arsenal's Annual General Meeting on Gallic influence in Arsenal's £500,000 purchase of Nicolas Anelka from Paris St Germain.

'Anelka knows he is the No. 1 choice for me.'

19 September 1998 – in praise of Arsenal's teenage striker.

'He is not the type of person the media represent at all. He is not an arrogant guy. He is reliable and shy, much more sensitive than people think. I sometimes put myself in his position and he is amazing for a twenty-year-old. He doesn't drink; he doesn't smoke; he is at training every day; he has played nearly every game this season. That deserves a lot of respect.'

30 April 1999 – further thoughts on Anelka, before it became clear that he was determined to leave Arsenal.

'[Ray] Parlour gets stronger when others get more tired.'

25 March 1999 – on the one-time drinking buddy of Tony Adams whose game was transformed under Wenger's new diet and fitness regime.

'For me, he [Parlour] is a real Arsenal man – a regular performer who offers the team so much with his stamina and strength.'

29 October 2001 – and more on the Romford-born Arsenal favourite.

'You need strong characters like Adams, Bould, Keown, Winterburn, Dixon, Seaman.'

28 March 1998 – name-checking the defensive line-up he inherited and retained in the years that followed.

'AC Milan, with Franco Baresi, Alessandro Costacurta, Paolo Maldini and Mauro Tassotti were successful for five or six years but these players [the Arsenal defence] have been together for ten years.'

10 April 1998 – recalling the defence of one of the great continental teams, which once went a whole season unbeaten in the top Italian division.

'So many people told me that I had to change the defenders, but they are still there today and they helped us do the Double.'

7 August 1998.

'It doesn't matter how good your team is. If you can't rely on your keeper you simply won't succeed.'

30 September 1998 – praising Arsenal goalkeeper David Seaman.

'Steve and Nigel are like two good bottles of French red wine. The older they get, the better they are.'

14 February 1998 – on vintage thirtysomethings Bould and Winterburn.

'The defence can go on for at least another season.'

18 May 1999 – signing Bould, Adams and Winterburn on new one-year contracts.

'Tony Adams has a big influence because not only is he a good individual player but he is a very good team player. He is very sensitive and can feel what is happening in the team.'

3 October 1997.

'[Adams is] a better player with the ball than I thought he was. All the defenders are better players on the ball than I thought they were. Bould as well. Keown as well. Of course Dixon and Winterburn, you know, they had to be able to play. But on the ball the central defenders are better than I thought.'

28 March 1998.

'When I first came to Arsenal, I realised the back four were all university graduates in the art of defending. As for Tony Adams, I consider him to be a doctor of defence. He is simply outstanding.'

10 April 1999 – a studious analysis of the Arsenal defence.

'We have to forget Tony Adams because Tony Adams is unique. You will not just find a Tony Adams around the corner.'

20 July 2002, and Tony Adams's retirement looms.

'Tony Adams is no longer an Arsenal player.'

5 August 2002, and final confirmation of Adams's departure after nineteen years as an Arsenal player.

Double 1

When the 1997–98 season began, many Arsenal supporters had high hopes for their team in the domestic campaign to come. Tony Adams still led a mighty defence of Englishmen, while the overseas signings like Petit and Overmars promised a new creativity in attack. And there was also a sense of expectation surrounding Arsène Wenger himself, whose way of doing things had been a breath of fresh air, gusting through the marble halls of Highbury.

But not even the most die-hard fan could honestly anticipate the Double success that lay ahead for Wenger's team. Over the previous five seasons, the Premiership title had been claimed on all but one occasion by Manchester United, who had twice added the FA Cup to claim the Double. For many commentators, the 1997–98 season promised nothing but more of the same United dominance, to the dismay of some.

But others dared to suggest that Manchester United might be knocked off their perch. In April 1997, Alex Ferguson was clearly rattled by his first media squabble with Wenger. More significantly, that summer, United's talismanic captain Eric Cantona announced his sudden retirement from football. In the season that followed, it would be another Frenchman who made the greatest contribution to success at the Double, as a supercharged Arsenal team put together a sizzling run of springtime victories.

'A strong team is there in March and April.'

24 September 1997 – after a good start to the new season, Arsenal's manager looks ahead to springtime, when his innovations in changing a player's diet and fitness regime would give his team an advantage over their rivals.

'I resent, at the moment, that everyone seems to think United are the only team in the country.'

7 November 1997 – prior to the Highbury encounter with Manchester United.

'This was such an important result psychologically ... I'm sure there will have been managers celebrating all over the country when Platt scored.'

9 November 1997 – after the Highbury encounter with Manchester United which was won by Arsenal with a late header from David Platt.

'At the moment it is just a dream to beat United; they are just too good.'

1 December 1997 – surely playing mind games, despite trailing United in the Premiership table. But, even with victory over Alex Ferguson's team, Arsenal had had a poor November, and not for the last time.

'David Seaman is the best goalkeeper I have worked with. His physical presence makes it very difficult for him to be beaten at penalties. There is a psychological factor for players who face him.'

14 January 1998 – after goalkeeping heroics from Seaman enable Arsenal to negotiate an FA Cup penalty shoot-out at Port Vale.

'We are still eight points away from Manchester United with a game in hand … you never know, if they have a real bad time and we have a real good time, it's not impossible.'

31 January 1998 – still trailing in the Premiership, but closing. The eight-point gap had earlier been thirteen.

'We look a real team now.'

14 March 1998 – after a 1–0 win at Old Trafford makes Arsenal the clear title favourites. Spring has sprung, and Arsenal are there or thereabouts, but not there yet.

'We will need all of our famous Arsenal spirit … this [game] against West Ham is super-important.'

16 March 1998 – prior to the FA Cup quarter-final replay which Arsenal would once again win on penalties.

'We shall take every game as it comes.'

31 March 1998 – now who's talking clichés after Arsenal's 1–0 Premiership win at Bolton?

'We have no negative thoughts at this time.'

11 April 1998 – a post-match comment after a 3–1 win over Newcastle, Arsenal's fifth successive Premiership victory.

'Every manager dreams of scoring many goals so I would
be stupid not to be happy today.'

**18 April 1998 – Arsenal had just extended their winning run to
seven with a 5–0 win over Wimbledon, who had given up their
contention for the Premiership title as a result.**

'I'm happy with the players I have.'

**25 April 1998 – after another 2–0 win, this time at Barnsley,
had added to Arsenal's chances of winning the title.**

'We have to be ruthless now, very professional,
determined and concentrated. We are in the last 100
yards. We have got to keep our concentration and not
become relaxed … We are fighting for a championship.
We are not in a dream world.'

**29 April 1998 – prior to the game with Derby, in which a ninth
successive victory would leave Arsenal needing just one more
win from three games to be champions.**

DOUBLE 1

'This has to be my best moment in football because, since December, we did not lose a game.'

3 May 1998 – after Arsenal's 4–0 victory over Everton. It was Arsenal's tenth win in a row and secured the Premiership title ...

'I'm very happy because we had a combination of exciting, entertaining football and efficiency.'

... in some style ...

'As it got closer I felt that if we didn't win it now everybody would come back and make the point again that a foreigner cannot win the championship.'

... to the delight of a Frenchman ...

'When we were thirteen points behind I felt we couldn't do it. I felt the championship was over. Of course, I couldn't say it, but because Manchester United are such a strong side I could not see us overtaking them.'

... fully appreciative of his team's achievement.

'It's an unbelievable achievement.'

16 May 1998 – after the 2–0 FA Cup Final win over Newcastle at Wembley brings Arsenal only their second-ever Double.

Business

Arsenal's 1998 Double confirmed that Arsène Wenger possessed all the gifts required of a modern football manager. As a coach, he had built an attractive, cosmopolitan team on a solid English foundation, and he had broken Manchester United's dominance of the English game, at least temporarily.

By 1998, Wenger had also proved himself comfortable in his dealings with the media. He had also shown his abilities in the murky waters of football's transfer market, a perhaps unsurprising state of affairs for a man with a degree in economics.

Wenger's early years in England saw a number of high-quality players join Arsenal at relatively low prices, only to be sold on later at a huge profit. This money was more than useful to a club that lagged behind their rivals Manchester United in terms of economic power. But Wenger's own comments revealed that these big-money sales were not always what he would have wanted.

The departure of Nicolas Anelka proved especially irritating, as the teenage striker himself used media messages to signal his wish to leave Highbury. For Arsène Wenger, the Anelka transfer saga of 1999 only served to highlight issues of loyalty and greed within football as a whole, all of which could be contrasted with Wenger's own commitment to Arsenal.

'I have control over all football matters, over wages and renewing contracts ... if I did not have the freedom to decide what to do I would not have stayed.'

30 September 1997 – explaining his position as football *auteur*. .....

'I determine what is really important inside the club: to buy and sell, to decide who is surrounding the team.'

... much more than just a *gaffer*.

'My word is the same as my signature.'

5 December 1998 – to reassure Arsenal fans that he would be renewing his own contract as manager.

'It will definitely be done tomorrow. Basically it is already done because I've given my word and that is more important than my signature. But now it is 100 per cent.'

8 December 1998 – offering further reassurance on a contract which was duly signed.

'It's a gamble. But every transfer is. Football would be less interesting without such gambles.'

9 May 1997 – on buying 18-year-old Matthew Upson from Luton for a fee of £2,000,000.

'Anelka has no right to complain. He has not been harassed or blamed. Invoking the press to justify leaving the club is a bad reason. They will be worse anywhere else.'

May 1999 – in response to reported comments by Arsenal striker Nicolas Anelka in which he blamed the press for causing him 'enormous problems' that made him want to leave England.

'Leaving Arsenal would be an enormous strategic error.'

18 May 1999 – and more advice for his apparently troubled striker.

'Two weeks ago, I was sure Anelka was going to stay, but today I'm a little more pessimistic because he is showing a real determination to leave us.'

27 June 1999 – as the teenage Anelka openly pursued a move to a 'bigger' European club, to the increasing frustration of his manager.

'Here he was not a gamble. He could come on as a substitute and there would be little expectation. There they will expect caviar – not sausages.'

9 July 1999 – warning his wayward striker not to expect an easy life if he went to Italy.

'I told the boy he can sleep in only one bed and eat only three meals a day.'

More summer 1999 comments as Anelka's apparently huge financial demands enter the public domain.

'The player will go for our price, or he will go nowhere. It's already a robbery for me – a bank robbery if we have to be punished twice.'

31 July 1999 – as Wenger resigns himself to losing Anelka.

'Thierry Henry wants to play for us and that's very positive.'

1 August 1999 – as the possibility of an immediate replacement for Anelka emerges in the form of another Frenchman, then unsettled at Juventus.

'In the end … it was a question of selling the player or killing his career.'

2 August 1999 – after confirmation of Anelka's transfer to Real Madrid for £23 million. Three days later, Arsenal signed Thierry Henry for £8.5 million.

'We lost Anelka this season but the financial benefit was great. We could have said, "You have to stay in the reserves for four years to learn a lesson." But at some stage we had to respect the financial interest of the club today … we had to compromise a little.'

2 September 1999 – and still peeved by the 'Anelka affair'.

'When I sign a player for a long time, it always means I have a lot of confidence in his quality and his commitment to the club. We have no special problems with Marc Overmars. It was just things coming out in the newspapers … that's down to you.'

20 November 1999 – faced with the reported wish of another Arsenal player to leave the club.

'In Italy, they throw away as quickly as they buy.'

19 March 1999 – and more warnings about Italy in response to Emmanuel Petit's apparent desire to leave the Premiership in favour of Serie A.

'It is very difficult to stop players leaving if someone offers them three times as much [money].'

25 July 2000 – Wenger is resigned to losing both Overmars and Petit to Barcelona.

'I felt that unless Marc and Manu had the right commitment to Arsenal we couldn't keep them.'

3 August 2000 – after Petit and Overmars move to Spain.

'When I signed Petit, nobody knew him. He wasn't even a midfielder. And when it came to Overmars he had been on the market for five months and no other club wanted him.'

9 August 2000 – after the departure of Overmars and Petit, Wenger suggests that their combined sale value of £30 million might have been something to do with him.

'The current situation is that we expect Edu to play with us. We honestly believed he had a passport and so did the player himself. He would never have tried to come in if he had known the passport was false.'

15 July 2000 – as Arsenal's desire to acquire the Brazilian international Edu is thwarted when the player is turned back at Heathrow.

'Lyon have been able to buy Edmilson because their work permit rules are very different. In France, as soon as you are offered a job you automatically get a work permit. When we tried to buy him he was ineligible because he did not meet the criteria here. You could say that it is unfair, but it is just the facts that everywhere in Europe there are different rules concerning work permits.'

17 November 2000 – and enlightenment on the relative difficulties of bringing Brazilian players to clubs in France and England ...

'At the moment the deal for Edmilson is dead because we are trying to sort out the Edu problem and then after we will see what we can do.'

... as Wenger still maintains his ultimately successful pursuit of Edu.

'Signing him [Tomas Danilevicius] is no kind of problem, but getting a British work permit for him could be a big one.'

4 August 2000 – and Lithuanians, too, present problems for Arsène Wenger.

'I have never broken a contract and I have no intention of doing so now.'

2 March 2001 – in response to a suggestion that Wenger was about to quit Arsenal to join Overmars and Petit in Barcelona.

'Sol Campbell is a great player but he has said he will stay at Tottenham, so what can I do?'

14 March 2001 – Wenger admits he would be interested in signing England's finest defender were he to leave White Hart Lane.

'I have not agreed anything yet but I know in my mind what I'll do. It will take a maximum of two meetings to decide things. I say that because it always takes time. It's like a girl being told never to say "yes" on a first date.'

14 May 2001 – being perhaps a little coy on the subject of signing another contract extension.

'My commitment to this club has always been clear. Perhaps I am from a different generation, but I don't need to sign something – if I give my word, it's my word.'

22 November 2001 – vowing to remain at Highbury, without having yet signed a new contract. Two weeks later, Wenger made good on his word.

'I want to sign big players, but that does not necessarily mean they have to be big names.'

30 May 2001.

'I know how the transfer market works and I am not stupid enough to believe that people don't talk to players before they try to sign them.'

17 August 2001 – in response to rumours of an illicit contact between Manchester United and Patrick Vieira.

'We were very, very close to signing Patrick Kluivert before he went to Barcelona. But Milan changed the price at the last moment.'

28 September 1999 – and, this time, Arsenal miss out on a gifted Dutchman.

'He [Patrick Kluivert] will have to speak to Jesus. We cannot afford those wages.'

24 October 2003 – four years on, and this time Wenger balks at the apparent cost of paying Patrick Kluivert's wages demands. Eventually, with or without divine assistance, the Dutchman signed for Newcastle.

'We have started contract talks and I don't think there will be any problems there.'

21 August 2004 – eight days after Patrick Vieira reaffirms his Arsenal future, his manager begins to do the same.

'My contract is just a question now of fine details ... I am not worried about it all and I expect it will be extended for a few years.'

5 October 2004 – familiar reassurance for Arsenal fans on the subject of a third extension to his period at Arsenal. The signing of the contract was announced 22 days later, and Wenger was now committed to Arsenal until 2008.

'You are always offered players by agents. You meet an agent and he offers you fifty players in half an hour.'

4 February 2005 – on the enduring reality of the 21st-century football agent.

Lamentations 1

No tournament signifies the boom in modern club football more than the UEFA Champions League. Huge TV fees have meant that every top club in Europe wants to be in the competition and, from 1998 onwards, Arsène Wenger's Arsenal duly qualified for the tournament on an annual basis.

But teams no longer had to be domestic champions to enter the Champions League, as Arsenal fans could appreciate in the three years that followed their Double triumph. In 1999, 2000 and 2001, Arsenal finished runners-up to Manchester United. Worse still, only in 1999 was the race remotely close, and Wenger's comments of the time reveal an almost distraught manager whose team were so near to and yet so far from repeating their successes of 1998.

In Europe, too, Arsenal were overshadowed by Alex Ferguson's team, whose Treble-securing Champions League victory of May 1999 contrasted sharply with Arsenal's first-round exit from the competition six months previously.

Another early exit followed in 1999–2000 and, though both failures were blamed on an ill-judged decision to play 'home' games at Wembley, the return to Highbury did nothing to bring European silverware to the club trophy room. For Arsène Wenger, success in Europe has always proved elusive and in England, too, his team struggled to follow up their remarkable achievements of 1998.

'Playing at Wembley will have an effect on the team because it is something unusual and exciting.'

25 September 1998 – looking forward to big European nights at England's national stadium.

'It was difficult going into a game like this without Dennis Bergkamp, Tony Adams and Marc Overmars. Then we lost Nicolas Anelka today with an infected foot. People keep saying I should buy more strikers but to cover a situation like this I would need to buy ten.'

4 November 1998 – after an injury-ravaged Arsenal side go down to defeat in Kiev.

'Perhaps we gave the fans too much last season. If you eat caviar every day, sometimes it is difficult to come back to sausages and mash.'

29 November 1998 – at the end of a difficult November at home and abroad.

'We knew it would be difficult. We knew there would be potential problems in November, but not as bad as it is.'

6 December 1998 – further reflections on a month that saw Arsenal win just one game out of seven.

'Panathinaikos played much better at Wembley than they did in Athens. In fact, every team that has come to Wembley has lifted their game because every team loves to play there.'

9 December 1998 – on a short-lived Champions League campaign which saw Arsenal pick up only four points out of nine at 'home'.

'It's impossible to say whether or not we would have qualified had we not played at Wembley.'

11 December 1998.

'We have accepted he [Dennis Bergkamp] will not step on to an aircraft again.'

10 September 1999 – on the continuing problem of Dennis Bergkamp's fear of flying. At that very moment, the aerophobe Dutchman was midway through a car journey from London to Florence to make a rare away appearance in a European game.

'If they [Barcelona] run after the ball they can slowly kill you. It's like drowning, you cannot do anything about it.'

28 September 1999 – prior to a Champions League encounter with the Catalan giants …

'How do you stop Rivaldo? You try and buy him before Wednesday.'

… and Wenger suggests an unlikely means of coping with Barcelona's gifted Brazilian.

'I expect to be under pressure, but only for short spells, and then it is intense. They are like snakes; they have spurts and in five minutes they can kill you.'

27 October 1999 – ahead of the decisive Champions League game against Fiorentina – at Wembley.

'We lost. We don't know why, but we lost. That's the reality now. We can't change it and we have to cope with that.'

27 October 1999 – after a venomous strike from Fiorentina's Gabriel Batistuta had eliminated Arsenal from the Champions League for another year.

'We have to think about why we have got nothing [from the Champions League] … We are certainly missing something.'

29 October 1999 – a return to Highbury is surely the answer.

'Although I defended the board's decision to play our Champions League games at Wembley, I have to concede now it was a mistake.'

25 November 1999 – Indeed. Arsenal's entry into that season's UEFA Cup appeared to be little consolation at the time.

'I thought we were stronger – strong enough to do it ... In fairness, it was a mistake. I didn't want to blame Wembley and use it as an excuse; I know how it is in England if you say something like that.'

Further reflections on an ill-fated decision.

'Usually we create chances and don't score, but today we just didn't create chances.'

9 January 1999 – a bad day up front in a tedious 0–0 with Liverpool.

'The two teams are very close to each other. It was a smashing game and in the end the luckiest won.'

14 April 1999 – after Ryan Giggs's extra-time wonder goal secures Manchester United a 2–1 victory in an epic FA Cup semi-final replay.

'This is a crucial night in the Premiership.'

5 May 1999 – before Arsenal's third from last game of the season against Spurs, with a victory essential to stay level on points with Manchester United at the top. Arsenal won 3–1 to take the Premiership race into the final week.

'It's unbelievable that we made so many chances and did not score. We are guilty of not taking our chances.'

11 May 1999 – after a 1–0 defeat by Leeds in the team's penultimate game of the season that proved decisive in Arsenal's failure to retain their Premiership title.

'They [Manchester United] are in the driving seat, but they can still lose it. Everybody expects Man United to win it now, so I would say there's already more pressure on them.'

14 May 1999 – Wenger resorts to mind games in advance of the final day of the Premiership season ...

'We haven't lost against Chelsea or Manchester United, and with our defence that should win the championship.'

... and ponders on what ought to be.

'We got the same number of points as last season and had a better defensive record but still we did not win [the Premiership].'

16 May 1999 – and a final-match victory is not enough to prevent the Premiership returning to Manchester United, whose players now stood on the brink of completing a season of unprecedented success.

'When they won the Treble, they seemed to have somebody upstairs who decided to give them all three.'

Later attestation of divine involvement in Manchester United's glories of 1999.

'We lost the title at the beginning of the [1998–99] season. Or rather we lost it twice. Once at the start because we picked up only 10 points out of the first 21, and the second time at Leeds.'

6 August 1999 – a new season looms, but Wenger still cannot help looking back.

LAMENTATIONS 1

'This defeat is not only a psychological blow, it is also a mathematical blow.'

22 August 1999 – Arsenal 1 Manchester United 2 = 3 points for United, 0 for Arsenal!

'The fixtures are an absolute joke. That was our third major game in seven days.'

28 August 1999 – a 2–0 defeat at Liverpool adds up to a bad start to the 1999–2000 season. Alex Ferguson was unlikely to sympathise.

'I felt the boys fought hard and showed some great quality. If one team should have won it, it was us.'

30 November 1999 – Arsenal go out of the League Cup on penalties to Middlesbrough.

'I'm upset every time we lose and this is no exception.'

19 January 2000 – Arsenal go out of the FA Cup on penalties to Leicester.

'We have to go there to win but it is crucial we don't lose because then we will be in dreamland if we think we can win the title.'

21 January 2000 – in advance of a game at Old Trafford. The game would finish 1–1, and Premiership paradise would be postponed, at least for a while.

'That's it for us and the championship. We can forget about Manchester United. The championship is played in England, not dreamland.'

5 February 2000 – dreamland again after a nightmare 2–1 defeat by Bradford leaves Arsenal hopelessly adrift of Manchester United in the league table.

'Since I've been in football, when you don't win, people always say, "Do they want it enough?" It's the same old story.'

13 February 2000 – after a 1–0 defeat against Liverpool leaves Arsenal with only the UEFA Cup to play for.

LAMENTATIONS 1

'They [Manchester United] had everything going for them, the championship was organised for them. They had a winter break, didn't play in the FA Cup and could then play their games in hand on FA Cup days.'

29 April 2000 – Wenger reflects with some bitterness on another Premiership title for his greatest rivals. United's absence from that season's FA Cup was also commented upon by Wenger on a number of other occasions.

'It's very disappointing because this is the third cup we have missed this season through penalty shoot-outs. We lost in the FA Cup and the Worthington Cup in that way too, and it is very difficult to take.'

17 May 2000 – after the UEFA Cup Final defeat completed a hat-trick of penalty losses during 1999–2000, with Arsenal left unhappy at the referee's decision to take the penalties in front of the Turkish supporters ...

'Nobody has seen this toss of the coin which is supposed to have happened.'

... which was apparently a matter of plain bad luck.

'It's always going to be a struggle to keep up with them [Manchester United] until we have our new stadium. At the moment they have 30,000 more people than us going into their stadium and that means 30,000 times more commercial potential.

21 July 2000 – Highbury is no longer big enough for Arsenal's ambitions, and plans for a new 60,000 capacity stadium at nearby Ashburton Grove are still just plans.

'We don't seem to have the kind of players who can force a goal through just strength to get us out of a situation when we have a bad day now and then.'

11 November 2000 – after a goalless draw with Derby County.

'Their [Everton's] players get paid at the end of every month, so I wasn't surprised to find that they could play football.'

18 November 2000 – after a 2–0 defeat at Goodison Park that surprised some Arsenal fans, if not necessarily the team manager.

'I'm not down at all. I just feel that when you see your team giving everything you want them to be rewarded … if you can find a manager in the world who leads 2–0 at that level and is happy when he comes out with a 2–2, I would like to be introduced to him.'

5 December 2000 – Arsenal throw away a lead in a crucial Champions League, second-phase game with Bayern Munich. Despite this, Arsenal did advance to the quarter-finals of that year's competition.

'We were not good enough.'

23 December 2000 – to the point after a Christmas thrashing by Liverpool.

'You can dream about how good you are but the table tells you the truth.'

1 January 2001 – and more Premiership gloom in the New Year, as Arsenal lose to Charlton.

'It seems we are not able to score a goal just through commitment or full aggression. We are always looking to score from the perfect pass. At the moment I would be happy with some scrappy goals.'

20 January 2001 – reflecting on another frustrating, goalless afternoon at Leicester. Some Arsenal fans would argue that this problem has never been fully resolved.

'I have problems to explain why the season has gone the way it has; it just looks to me that they [Manchester United] have done nothing special but they are thirteen points ahead.'

23 February 2001 – apparently at a loss to explain Manchester United's dominance in that season's Premiership. Still, Wenger's team would soon have the opportunity to reduce their deficit to ten points at the home of their great rivals.

'I have had worse experiences, but the size of the score makes this a very bad one.'

25 February 2001 – Manchester United 6 Arsenal 1 ...

'We are not into March yet and it hurts me that the title is already over. It's not good for the league, and I'm not proud of that.'

... and, with United sixteen points ahead, Wenger concedes the title to Alex Ferguson's team for the third successive year.

'I congratulate United ... we have to accept that they are a better team ... the table doesn't lie.'

14 April 2001 – after a feeble 3–0 home defeat by Middlesbrough guaranteed Manchester United's title with a month to spare. But Arsenal were already in the final of the FA Cup, and were still in the 2000–01 Champions League ...

'We now have to face the reality that we are out, no matter how unhappy we are.'

... until defeat by Valencia on 17 April 2001.

'The away record does not bother me. We have the character and determination to do well away in the Champions League and I hope tomorrow will show me right not to be bothered.'

20 November 2001 – before a European game at Deportivo la Coruña, in response to the observation that Arsenal had lost seven of their previous eight away games in the Champions League. Twenty-four hours later, it was eight out of nine.

'It was a very sad night for the whole squad. It was terrible.'

8 December 2002 – Wenger still recalls his April 2001 defeat in Spain.

'We feel guilty because we should have scored the goals and we gave some cheap goals away. We should have won the game. Nobody is to blame but as a team we are hugely disappointed.'

13 May 2001 – after Arsenal contrive to lose the FA Cup Final to Liverpool despite leading after 83 minutes.

LAMENTATIONS 1

'You expect too much of us … it's not just Arsenal's responsibility to chase Manchester United.'

14 April 2001.

'I still believe in this team.'

14 May 2001 – as Arsenal near the end of a third successive season without a trophy.

Discipline 1

By the summer of 2001, Wenger's Arsenal had established an unwanted reputation as a 'nearly' team after three successive runners-up finishes in the Premiership and two Cup Final defeats. And, in the opinion of many commentators, Arsenal were also a 'dirty' team, with much evidence to support the assertion.

From the beginning of the Wenger era, Arsenal players have made regular appearances in referees' notebooks, and the tally of red cards received has become an ongoing joke within the English game. Crucially, Wenger himself has been accused of making light of misconduct by his players, most notably his combative French midfielder, Patrick Vieira.

Arsène Wenger's defences of his players have become famous, or infamous, depending on your viewpoint. In public, at least, the Arsenal team manager has demonstrated a fierce loyalty to his players, seemingly regardless of their on-field conduct. In the minds of many critics, this is a loyalty whose blindness is far from virtuous.

It is an allegation that is hard to refute entirely. Arsène Wenger may be one of the most visionary coaches ever to work in English football, but there can be no doubt that, on certain occasions, the gift of sight seems to depart him.

'Frankly, I did not see what happened.'

19 October 1996 – after Coventry goalkeeper Steve Ogrizovic is taken off bleeding as a result of a challenge by Arsenal's Ian Wright that looked malicious to those who did see it. This was Arsène Wenger's second game in charge at Arsenal and, since Ian Wright was not dismissed for his clash with Ogrizovic, the red-card count under Wenger still stood at zero.

'When you argue with the referee, you are not concentrating on the game.'

22 November 1996.

'It seems that we have a lot of red and yellow cards but I am sure that some of them are not deserved.'

21 December 1996 – after Ian Wright is sent off at Nottingham Forest, already the third such dismissal of the Wenger era.

'Too many red cards, but I cannot condemn the behaviour of my team because, as I explained to you before, the three red cards we got before we didn't deserve.'

1 January 1997 – when John Hartson becomes the fourth, dismissed for dissent in a New Year's Day clash with Middlesbrough ...

'It's always stupid to talk to the referee.'

... though perhaps only the first in Wenger's mind.

'It was stupid for Ian [Wright] and Tony [Adams] to get yellow cards. They should know not to argue with the referee.'

16 September 1997 – again censorious of dissent by his own players ...

'Patrick Vieira's yellow card for a trip in the last minute was also unnecessary.'

... and not only dissent, as Arsenal's manager shows his frustration after a UEFA Cup defeat by Salonika in Greece.

'I don't criticise referees.'

11 January 1997 – after a 1–0 defeat at Sunderland in which Dennis Bergkamp is sent off.

'It is a great gesture by Fowler and I would like to give him an award of fair play. But if he got that I would also have to give the referee an award for stupidity.'

24 March 1997 – commenting on Liverpool's Robbie Fowler's appeals to the referee not to give a penalty against Arsenal's David Seaman. The referee took no notice. The non-critical Wenger didn't.

'I don't want to talk about the referee because I want to sit on the bench in the next game.'

28 September 1999 – an excellent 1–1 draw in Barcelona is marred by five bookings for Arsenal players, and the Arsenal manager seems to suggest that they might just have been ... unjustified?

'I didn't really see what happened.'

15 March 1997 – after a game at Southampton in which Patrick Vieira appeared to strike Matthew Le Tissier, unseen by the referee as well as Wenger.

'[Emmanuel Petit] wanted to protect himself as the referee was running his way.'

26 October 1997 – explaining why Arsenal's French midfielder felt it necessary to lay hands on referee Paul Durkin during a game with Aston Villa. Durkin apparently interpreted the incident differently from Arsène Wenger and sent Petit off for violent conduct.

'Grimandi made a head movement towards him but didn't touch him.'

20 December 1998 – could an Arsenal defender really have *head-butted* an opponent?

'I like players who put their foot in and behave aggressively on the field. But I don't like cheats.'

31 December 1998 – Wenger resorts to the C-word after Patrick Vieira is dismissed having lashed out at the close attentions of Charlton Athletic's Neil Redfearn ...

DISCIPLINE 1

'My thought is that Patrick didn't deserve to be sent off
and that Redfearn cheated the referee.'

**... who was wholly the guilty party, according to the Arsenal
manager, at least.**

'We live in a democracy and Alan Curbishley has every
right to have a different opinion.'

**8 January 1999 – after a week of open media squabbling about
the Vieira–Redfearn encounter on which Charlton's manager
expressed a different view to that held by Arsène Wenger.**

'I did not see what happened.'

**22 August 1999 – this time Vieira is deemed lucky to escape
punishment for butting Roy Keane of Manchester United ...**

'Roy Keane is not especially an angel.'

**... prompting comment on the character of the Manchester
United player.**

'Patrick's behaviour was unacceptable and is something we do not condone.'

5 October 1999 – after an ill-tempered game in which West Ham's Neil Ruddock taunted Vieira throughout, and the Arsenal player eventually responded by spitting at his persecutor. The incident occurred shortly after Vieira had been sent off for a second bookable foul on Paolo di Canio, at which point Ruddock ran forty yards across the pitch to goad his rival for a final time ...

'It was cheating by di Canio ... He dived for Vieira's first yellow card and again for the sending off, so Patrick was very upset.'

... leaving Wenger sympathetic to his own player.

'Why will Patrick be punished? Because of TV evidence. So why are the provokers not punished by TV evidence as well? Just because they spoke nicely the next day to the newspapers?'

11 October 1999 – after some holier-than-thou media comments by the far-from-saintly Ruddock in the aftermath of the Vieira episode.

DISCIPLINE 1

'For the last two weeks he's [Vieira's] been depicted as a super gangster. But today he was a normal human being again.'

16 October 1999 – Wenger still muses on off-field matters after Vieira helps Arsenal to a 4–1 win over Everton. But Vieira now faced a disciplinary hearing concerning the West Ham game which would also consider his apparent swearing at a policeman.

'I have said all I want to say about Ruddock.'

28 October 1999 – in bitter mood after Vieira receives a six-match ban for his conduct during the West Ham game ...

'The punishment is very severe. Patrick answered a policeman who touched him from behind and swore.'

... so that's two matches for bad-mouthing a copper and four matches for spitting.

'He shouldn't have done that, but he deserves a lot of respect for his reaction. He accepted the punishment with dignity. He didn't come out and say it's not justified; he didn't cry. He said, "I made a mistake and I will show I can change." And that's what he has done.'

6 April 2000 – Wenger reflects on the Vieira–Ruddock–Plod shenanigans.

'The best discipline is to score goals.'

26 October 1997 – spinning an answer to questions of Arsenal's disciplinary record.

'To call us a dirty side is unbelievable. It seems to us that it is always Arsenal players who are being watched and their every move examined.'

11 January 1999.

'We are not a dirty side. In fact, we are a nice side, too nice at times.'

25 January 1999 – after Emmanuel Petit receives the nineteenth red card of the Wenger era in a 2–1 FA Cup victory at Wolves ...

DISCIPLINE 1

'I don't know what Emmanuel [Petit] did to get sent off.'

... leaving the manager mystified once again. (Petit was dismissed for foul and abusive language directed at a linesman.)

'Every team enjoys feeling like it's us against the world.'

21 January 2000 – evidence of a bunker mentality at Arsenal encouraged by the team manager.

'For me it was clear. Maybe if you had different glasses you didn't see it.'

7 November 1999 – questioning the vision of referee David Elleray after he failed to punish Spurs' Tim Sherwood for an apparent elbow on Emmanuel Petit during a rare Arsenal defeat at Tottenham, though the Harrow schoolmaster did give marching orders to Arsenal's Freddie Ljungberg and Martin Keown.

'Maybe I should invite some referees to explain why we have so many sendings-off. Perhaps a good dinner could solve the problem.'

1 April 2000 – pondering a culinary solution to Arsenal's disciplinary troubles after Oleg Luzhny receives Arsenal's 28th red card in less than four seasons.

'I wouldn't like to think that his [Vieira's] reputation is affecting referees.'

19 August 2000 – after Vieira is, perhaps, harshly sent off in a season opener at Sunderland.

'I did not see the incident with Simeone, but maybe he caught an elbow in the eye.'

18 October 2000 – after a bad-tempered Champions League game in Rome, in which Lazio's Diego Simeone is left bloodied after a clash with Arsenal's Gilles Grimandi.

DISCIPLINE 1

'It was FIFA Fair Play Day and I feared the worst.
Sometimes these occasions can bring a surprise.'

**21 October 2000 – in droll mood, after Arsenal return to West
Ham for a game in which no red cards are awarded, evidently
to the surprise of the Arsenal manager.**

Wisdom

Arsène Wenger has defended his players in all circumstances, with or without the aid of myopia, and he has been eloquent in doing so. Indeed, this cultured, reflective eloquence stands in sharp contrast with the brute force occasionally deployed by some members of his Arsenal teams.

Wenger's obvious intelligence suggests that he has defended Arsenal players as part of a wholly deliberate strategy of team management conceived and executed by the manager himself. There can be no doubt that Arsène Wenger has studied deeply the psychology of winning within a competitive team environment, and his sometimes blind loyalty to his players can be understood as part of a coherent strategy for football success.

And it is the game of football that has prompted Monsieur Wenger's most insightful observations. Right from the start of his spell at Highbury, the Arsenal manger has chosen his words to express his deeply-held views on the game that he lives and breathes.

Wenger's relationship with football is, then, a serious one, but his comments on the game have also revealed a cheeky, diffident sense of humour that has delighted both Arsenal fans and neutrals alike. For season after season, the French manager has offered the English football public a selection of *bons mots* that reveal not only a well-considered philosophy of sport, but also a philosophy of life.

'Don't allow yourself to be manipulated by a minority just because a few people are shouting the loudest. Names die; fame can be short term. It is the quality of your work which can survive the longest.'

September 1996 – from a public message to Arsenal fans following news of his appointment as team manager.

'For a professional player, it's not normal to get up in the morning and say, "OK, let's go on with the fight." You need a special attitude. Winners are those who are able to do it.'

22 November 1996.

'The real revelation of a player's character is not in his social life, but in how he plays ... Sometimes if a player is really dirty on the field but outside in life he is so nice, at important times in his life he will become like he is on the field.'

24 November 1996, on the general subject of man and footballer ...

'You can only be successful if you concentrate on your strong points. Nobody can be perfect. If you have one strong point in life you are already lucky. Why try to destroy it? Just play with it.'

... and the specific subject of the man and footballer Ian Wright.

'On the last weekend of the championship, every team should play on the same day and at the same time, otherwise it would be unfair.'

4 April 1997 – in response to Manchester United's pleas for an extension to the season, a comment that opened up the very first 'mind games' dispute between Arsène Wenger and Alex Ferguson.

'It's not because you know that you have to win that you win. It's best, first of all, to love what you do. And if you want to love what you do it must not be compulsory; it must be something you want to achieve and you enjoy.'

24 September 1997.

'You cannot play well when you are unhappy, that's for sure.'

4 October 1997.

'When you get up every morning and you cannot walk, you cannot feel like jumping around and kicking the ball.'

20 February 1998 – wise words indeed on the subject of player injuries.

'A winner never really loses sight of what he wants and what is important.'

26 February 1999.

'You are a winner or not a winner, and, if you are a winner, it's important for you to win throughout your whole life.'

3 March 1999 – and more on the victorious character.

'That's when you respect players, when they are stars on the field and men outside.'

11 April 1999 – praising Dennis Bergkamp, another man and footballer.

'The true champions are those who, once they reach the summit, want to stay there.'

3 January 1999 – on the subject of Arsenal's Double-winning World Cup winner, Emmanuel Petit.

'A competitive guy who does not have competition gets sick.'

14 April 1999 – on Petit's return to the Arsenal side after his third suspension of the season.

'When you finish one point behind after 38 games it is like losing a marathon by a yard.'

17 May 1999 – speaking from still-raw personal experience.

'If you keep scoring late, you believe you can score late.'

**25 September 1999 – after an 86th-minute goal from Kanu
beats Watford 1–0.**

'Consistency gives you a chance to win something.
Potential, nothing.'

20 November 1999.

'I love life in England, especially with Arsenal, but you can
find some qualities in Japan which you maybe have missed
in England. There is 100 per cent dedication, a respect by
people for one another and a strong feeling of security.'

**2 May 2000 – Wenger paints a favourable impression of the
country where he worked before coming to Arsenal.**

'When you don't win you are responsible for so many
unhappy people. Sometimes it's better not to think about
it because it could damage your life too much.'

11 August 2000.

'Sometimes, when you can't take your chances, you have to make sure you win 1–0.'

10 November 2002 – after a game against Newcastle whose scoreline was certainly familiar to seasoned Arsenal fans.

'The FA have shown strong support for Glenn [Hoddle] and they are right. You cannot allow the papers to rule the decisions of the FA.'

20 October 1998 – praising English football's governing body for sticking with the national team manager after another underachievement at the 1998 World Cup.

'Maybe he's not been very subtle, but I know he's not a bad guy with people who are disabled.'

30 January 1999 – and changed times for Glenn Hoddle, who found himself vilified for outlining some of his spiritual beliefs. These included his opinion that disabled people were suffering for the misdeeds of a previous lifetime.

'He [Hoddle] was sacked for his beliefs. Still, 500 years ago you could be burnt at the stake for that. At least now you are only sacked. Things have improved a little bit.'

5 February 1999 – Wenger reacts to Hoddle's dismissal as England manager for stating his views on reincarnation. ...

'Can you imagine this happening if England had won the World Cup?'

... with the suggestion that football matters might have played a part in Hoddle's sacking. ...

'What I've seen recently hasn't put me in that sort of mood [to consider taking the England job].'

... and ruling himself out as Hoddle's replacement.

'What happened to him was not a football problem.'

9 April 1999 – a final word on the hounding from office of a public figure for expressing his private beliefs.

'I prefer things to remain in the hands of football, not with the police. It's difficult as sometimes during matches you say more than you think in the heat of the game. You cannot go to jail for that.'

22 December 2000 – more wisdom after a Champions League game in Rome, during which Patrick Vieira was racially abused by Lazio's Sinisa Mihajlovic, leading to police investigation of the latter's conduct.

'We don't live in a world where everybody has to be nice. We live in a world where you have to perform on the field and, as long as the players do that, I'm happy.'

19 February 2001.

'I know that patience is not the biggest quality in our society any more.'

5 March 2001 – in response to Sylvain Wiltord's public whingeing at his failure to establish himself as a guaranteed first-choice Arsenal player.

'The Germans are the Germans.'

13 March 2001 – scoffing at suggestions that Bayern Munich might be ill prepared for their forthcoming Champions League game with Arsenal.

'[Married players] have more emotional stability unless they are married to a nightmare.'

9 April 1999 – espousing the benefits of, er, espousal ... but with one wholly sensible reservation.

'Part of leadership is respect and you don't get that kind of respect at twenty or 22. You get it when everybody knows you have done it before.'

23 February 2001 – more valuable observations, though it should be pointed out that Tony Adams was still at the time Arsenal's captain, and had been since the age of twenty.

'It's a choice between a passionate life and a really quiet life and for me that's no choice. I came into this job so I could stay in football and I thought it would lead me to extreme emotions and tell me a lot about myself. I was not wrong. Maybe I will die two or three years earlier. Maybe ten. But I could also have died with a boring life.'

7 December 2001 – on signing a contract keeping him at Arsenal until 2005 ...

'No matter where you work in the world, if you get up in the morning and you're not happy to go to your job, it's not worth doing it.'

... presumably in anticipation of at least four more years of professional happiness.

'When you are 1–0 down, 40 minutes to go, with 10 men at an away ground, you need great, great strength.'

1 September 2002 – Patrick Vieira is sent off for the eighth time in England, but Arsenal still take a point at Stamford Bridge.

'You can be caught driving at 80mph on the motorway but it's not right if every day it is just you.'

9 September 2002 – suggesting Patrick Vieira was being consistently overpunished by English referees.

'It's not healthy to be negative. If today I am healthy, I know tomorrow I could die, but if I think like that there's more chance I will die.'

20 September 2002.

'It is a question of what you like most: vanilla or chocolate ice cream. Both are good. I just like vanilla more.'

10 December 2002 – on the relative merits of Premiership (Vanilla) and Champions League (Chocolate) football.

'I am always frustrated when my team doesn't win.'

27 February 2003.

'Would I compromise my principles? On occasions yes, as first and foremost I'm a winner, but long term that's not my attitude, or that of my players.'

2 March 2003 – the visionary confesses the need for pragmatism.

'Do people want me to say we cannot win it [the Premiership] when I know we can?'

6 March 2003 – responding to media comments about Arsenal's apparent overconfidence. Note that 'people' here means, most specifically, 'Alex Ferguson'. ...

'I speak the truth as I see it, so why lie?'

... prompting his rival to get all reasonable, perhaps.

'Talk in football is not so important. What is important is how well you play.'

5 March 2003 – as another spell of media jousting with Ferguson gets under way.

'There is only one good feeling and that's to be on top after the final whistle of the 38th game.'

3 April 2003.

'What looks dull and dark today might look bright tomorrow.'

26 April 2003 – after a 2–2 draw with Bolton whose bright side remained unperceived by Arsenal fans.

'Bolton being in the middle of the table is a bit like how we are at the top.'

20 December 2003 – eight months on, and Wenger offers an honest analysis of two Premiership clubs' ambitions after another hard-fought draw at the Reebok Stadium.

'Young boys make mistakes. But, if they don't learn, there's no future for them.'

4 April 2003 – responding to Arsenal player Jermaine Pennant's disciplinary problems with the England Under-21 squad.

'I am absolutely for the fact that you need strong punishments to get drugs out of the game.'

20 December 2000 – one of many public comments advocating a hard line against performance-enhancing drug-taking within football.

'I don't think Rio Ferdinand was doping. He doesn't need to dope to be a good player.'

19 March 2004 – expressing sympathy for Rio Ferdinand after the Manchester United and England defender receives an eight-month ban for missing a drugs test.

'We don't expect [Roy] Keane to help us win the title.'

21 February 2004 – in response to media comments from the Manchester United captain, apparently suggesting that Arsenal would win the 2003–04 title ...

'I read what Keane said and what I got out of his message was that he is not too much concerned by us but that he is more concerned by them.'

... comments duly dealt with by *spinmeister* Wenger.

'When you play your wife at tennis, you can love her to death but you still want to beat her.'

22 March 2004 – always competitive.

'I will always consider myself to have underachieved, because it is the way I am.'

20 October 2004 – but never satisfied.

'If you have quality and ability it doesn't matter – unless you have commitment and desire and go out and express yourself, you won't get anywhere.'

16 April 2004, after Arsenal's Thierry Henry scores four goals in a 5–0 defeat of Leeds United.

'When opposition can't compete technically, they compensate with commitment.'

27 September 2004 – after ninety minutes' commitment by Manchester City fails to prevent their losing at home to Arsenal.

'If you always envisage a disaster before a game, it's better you are not a manager because you die.'

10 December 2004 – reasons to be cheerful in advance of a top-of-the-table encounter with the newly credible title challengers Chelsea.

'Trophies are the consequence of our game.'

20 September 2002.

The Beautiful Game

George Graham's Arsenal team won trophies, and plenty of them. But they won few friends with a technically sound, yet suffocatingly defensive style of play. Graham's teams could be admired, but never loved, and the phrase '1–0 to the Arsenal' came to sum up the turgid footballing fare served up at Highbury around the turn of the 1990s.

Arsène Wenger's achievement has been to deliver even greater success with a far more modern kind of game. If Graham's teams were forged in the British industrial age, Wenger's teams have expressed the spirit of the space age with an exciting, forward-looking brand of football in which pace, movement and technique are harnessed together in an offensive team strategy.

This emphasis on lightning attack has been wholly Arsène Wenger's creation, and has delighted Arsenal fans who remember the old days at Highbury. Wenger's is a kind of football that, at its best, takes the breath away, and there can be no doubt that this transformation of a once-dour football team has been down to its manager's personal belief in just how beautiful the beautiful game can be.

'I like real, modern football. That means compact lines, of zones, of quick, coordinated movements with a good technique. I play 4-4-2 if I can. It's very adaptable because you can change easily to 4-3-3 or 4-5-1 … with three at the back you have to come a little deeper, and I like offensive football and winning the ball early. It is much more difficult to pressurise up the field with three at the back.'

22 September 1996 – and back to that first press conference.

'What is creative? To me, creative is scoring goals.'

24 November 1996 – *touché*.

'It is difficult to find players who can give key passes and score goals – they are rare in the world.'

4 February 1997.

'What motivates me is an ideal of thinking how football should be. And to try to get near this way of playing. And to try to improve all aspects of my personality that can help me get near this ideal way of playing football.'

13 September 1997.

'For me the most important thing is not the private lives of the players, it's not my concern. For me it's how much they love their job, and he loves his game. That's why he's a great player. It's always the same. You can speak about a player, but at the end of the day, does he really love to play? Does he really love the game? Could you call him tomorrow to come and play a game with friends? If he has that, for me, that's a characteristic of the big player; he loves to play.'

4 October 1997.

'You can never say when you score a great goal that it's unfair.'

21 October 1998 – on a fine diving header by Dennis Bergkamp against Dynamo Kiev, which came just a minute after Kiev were unlucky to have a 'goal' disallowed for offside.

'The first thing for a player is to perform well on the pitch and to give joy and happiness from what you do on the field.'

1 May 1999.

'When you are young and fit, you want big fields. When you are old and slow, you want narrow pitches.'

16 March 1998 – a possible explanation for the continuing success of Arsenal's ageing defence, at least in home games on the famously narrow Highbury pitch.

'[The Villa Park pitch] is the worst in the Premiership. There was no grass and today it was hard and bumpy.'

18 March 2001 – after a frustrating 0–0 draw at Aston Villa, Wenger suggests that football artists need a good canvas on which to paint.

'I will never walk away from football. I love football.'

9 July 1999.

THE BEAUTIFUL GAME

'We looked a hungry team, played a very creative game and had the right concentration for nearly ninety minutes. This is an important week for us and the target is to repeat it.'

20 November 1999 – after Arsenal turn on the style to thump Middlesbrough 5–1.

'Forwards have to be fresh. They have to do so much more running off the ball, trying to be creative, yet maybe only one in ten of those runs produces anything. It can be really exhausting.'

10 March 2000.

'I feel that Brazilians take around five or six months to develop in the English game.'

15 December 2000 – still endeavouring to sign Edu, presumably in time for the 2001–02 season.

'In football, you can never say never.'

22 December 2000 – ruling out buying Robbie Fowler. Or, at least, ruling out buying Robbie Fowler on 22 December 2000.

'You can't explain everything in football. It always surprises you.'

26 December 2000 – after Arsenal beat Leicester City 6–1 just three days after a 4–0 pasting at Liverpool.

'What you have to get out of every player is a servant for the team's vision and goals.'

30 December 2001 – the master's voice.

'When they have the ball, I can watch them for hours. Because it looks so classy, it's art. When football gets close to art and the communication between the players is right so that everybody does something intelligent when he has the ball, it becomes an art and it's that moment of beauty when you really enjoy to watch.'

On Real Madrid, European Cup winners in 2002 ...

'[Ronaldo is] the pepper in Real Madrid's sauce.'

... and spicy acclaim for their Brazilian superstar.

'When I see this team playing there are moments when I think that I would pay to watch them.'

September 2002 – on his own Arsenal eleven, at a time when their performances under Wenger were as compelling as any ever witnessed in the English game.

'We are playing great football, total football.'

28 September 2002 – Wenger compares his team with the greatest European teams of the past, specifically the Ajax team that won the European Cup three times in succession.

'The great teams like Real Madrid, Ajax of the Seventies and AC Milan have their names in history, not just because of the trophies they won, but the type of game they have played.'

26 February 2003 – more on the historic giants of European club football.

'They [Ajax] really had perfect players nearly everywhere on the field. At the time I thought, 'That is the sort of football I would like to play.'

9 March 2004 – Wenger again recalls the team led by the peerless Johan Cruyff ...

'We are far [from Ajax's achievements] because that team won everything in Europe.'

... while accepting that his own team still had some way to go in comparison.

'Would we beat Brazil? I don't know. Let's try and organise it – I'm sure we'd have a sell-out at Highbury.'

September 2002 – Arsenal still unbeaten all year, and no end to their manager's ambitions?

'A football team is like a beautiful woman. When you do not tell her, she forgets she is beautiful. It is the same with a team. When you do not tell them they are good, they can also forget.'

10 November 2002.

'We want to win with a style of play and a way of enjoying the game, to give people watching us something.'

26 February 2003.

'Trophies are not handed out for artistic impression.'

26 February 2003 – pointing out that style on its own is not enough for success.

'We want to be efficient, not ugly. I don't think we are the perfect team: there is still a lot we can improve. But, if you look at the teams who, historically, have been successful, they were never ugly.'

16 March 2003.

'Teams express the way the managers want to play football and what they want to come out of that side. Part of your personality is always in the team.'

16 April 2003.

'It's funny – you're living in a small world and you're not conscious at all that it goes out of Islington … you don't realise how big an impact it can have all over the world.'

24 February 2004.

'The best thing for a professional footballer [in England] is that when he goes out he doesn't see an empty seat. That to me is paradise.'

21 March 2004 – and heavenly praise for the English game, and its sell-out Premiership.

Double 2

For all his beliefs in the aesthetic qualities of beautiful football, Arsène Wenger has always understood that even the most attractive teams still need to win trophies. When the 2001–02 season began, Wenger knew only too well that his team had won nothing since 1997–98. Many commentators forecast another season of Manchester United domination to come, but the Arsenal manager appeared unruffled, and talked openly of new successes for his own team.

He had some grounds for optimism. Arsenal were now well established at a new state-of-the-art training centre, designed to Wenger's specifications. The Arsenal team also boasted a world-class striker in the person of Thierry Henry, as well as a new English player, Sol Campbell, signed on a free transfer from Tottenham in the summer of 2001.

The signing seemed to suggest that Arsenal had something to offer the best English defender in the game, but few predicted just how much Arsenal would achieve during Campbell's debut season at Highbury, with the notable exception of his manager. By May 2002, Arsène Wenger was able once more to enjoy the taste of success, achieved entirely on his own terms.

'I think we can stay at the top. Why not?'

15 September 2001 – a win at Fulham takes Arsenal to the summit of the Premiership, leaving their manager in bullish mood ...

'I don't want to be too negative about second place as many clubs would be happy with that, but, for me, it's important to win everything every season.'

... remarkably bullish, indeed, for a manager whose team had won nothing for three years.

'We got through with tremendous character, energy and belief. When you have those things, as well as talent, you always have a chance.'

9 December 2001 – after coming from 2–0 down to beat Aston Villa 3–2 with a last-minute winner from Thierry Henry ...

'This win is a sign of growing unity in the team which strikes me every day in training.'

... which augurs well for the remainder of the 2001–02 season ...

'The players want to be first and they believe they can win it [the title].'

... as Wenger now thinks of something better than a fourth successive second-place finish

'Revenge? No, because we look forwards, not backwards.'

25 January 2002 – looking ahead to an FA Cup fourth-round game against Liverpool, just eight months after the Anfield side had stunned Arsenal in the previous year's Cup Final.

'I've been spoiled in my time here but it was a dream goal.'

27 February 2002 – after a wonderful build-up leads to a sensational Henry goal in Arsenal's 4–1 victory at Bayer Leverkusen.

'I believe we can win the Treble.'

1 March 2002 – unbounded dreams of glory from Arsène Wenger ...

'We are not stupid and there is still a long way to go. But the spirit and determination are there. We are strong mentally and there is a realistic belief in the squad. Winning is a good habit.'

... in advance of a down-to-earth Premiership game at Newcastle.

'Unbelievable ... you're blessed when you come to a stadium and witness something like that.'

2 March 2002 – after a goal-of-the-season from Dennis Bergkamp secures a 2–0 win at St James' Park.

'We have the talent and the pace.'

1 April 2002 – after a 3–0 win over Charlton is secured within 25 minutes of the kick-off. This was the third successive Premiership game that Arsenal won 3–0, with eight of the nine goals scored in the first halves of the matches. Arsenal were indeed a team in a hurry.

'I did not see it – from the bench it's impossible to see what happened.'

24 April 2002 – Wenger vision failure, again, after a 2–0 victory over West Ham, in which an opening 'goal' by West Ham was controversially disallowed ...

'When the other team gets tired, we just are like a machine, coming on and coming, and coming again.'

... but nonetheless able to observe the orgasmic performance of his own team.

'We have things in our hands now. We have a great belief that we will do the Double.'

14 April 2002 – after an FA Cup semi-final victory over Middlesbrough. Arsenal were now out of Europe, but domestic domination was still within their grasp.

'I promised Richard [Wright] that I would play him in Cup games and I did it. But there is no pact; there is only one agreement here – to win all the trophies.'

1 May 2002 – in advance of the FA Cup Final, and Wenger gets serious about goalkeeping. In all Arsenal's Cup games thus far, reserve goalkeeper Richard Wright had worn the jersey. But, with the final beckoning, the Arsenal boss considered restoring his No. 1, David Seaman.

'It was important to win the first trophy so we can go to Old Trafford to win the second.'

4 May 2002 – after a 2–0 FA Cup Final victory over Chelsea secures the first half of a second Double. David Seaman kept the clean sheet.

'What relaxes me is knowing the effort the team is putting in. I have never had to ask myself this question this season. I can go home knowing this team will give their last drop of blood for me.'

8 May 2002 – Churchillian talk prior to the game at Old Trafford, where Arsenal needed just a draw to secure the Premiership title.

'I personally believe that what this team has achieved is tremendous and will remain in history. We have 84 points; we have played nineteen games away from home without losing one and we have scored in every game. The character of this team is extraordinary. This is not only a team of good players, it is a team of togetherness. We wanted there to be a shift of power. Winning it [the Premiership] almost felt natural, but I have lost a few times since then and realised how hard it is.'

8 May 2002 – after a 1–0 victory at Old Trafford brings Wenger a second Premiership crown ...

'It's difficult to explain. It's just a fact.'

... when he was asked why his Arsenal team had become the first side to go through a season unbeaten away from home ...

'We wanted there to be a shift of power and to bring the Premier League trophy back home. Now we want to win it again next season. Since I arrived at Arsenal, we have won the title twice and United have won it three times. So they are 3–2 ahead and now we want to equalise.'

... and Field Marshal Wenger surveys the strategic picture.

'Not only have we won the championship, we have won it in style.'

12 May 2002 – the achievement of a second Double sinks in.

'My team are hungry; they want to win more.'

11 August 2002 – after a new season begins with a 1–0 victory over Liverpool in the Community Shield.

'The record means that the team has consistency, quality, ambition and spirit.'

18 August 2002 – a 2–0 win over Birmingham is Arsenal's fourteenth successive Premiership victory, a record for the top flight.

'It's good to be top … it's where we feel comfortable.'

27 August 2002 – after a 5–2 win over West Bromwich puts the champions in a familiar position in the Premiership table.

DOUBLE 2

'If you look at the classification of the clubs in the world on results in 2002 in the European Cup, championships and domestic cups, we are No. 2 behind Real Madrid.'

15 September 2002 – Wenger calls on statistics to hint at his team's status within European football.

Arsenal Football Club

Modern professional football is a global business, and leading clubs such as Arsenal are huge commercial enterprises. But a football club is a very special kind of company. No matter how rich a club becomes, its identity continues in the relationship between the team and the supporters who remain the lifeblood of the game.

To be a fan of a football club is to engage in an essentially tribal activity whose lifelong nature transcends commercial notions of 'brand loyalty'. This is true in all major footballing nations but, in England, the individual supporting of a football club is built on uniquely historic traditions.

Arsenal fans are no exceptions to this rule, and it is one of Arsène Wenger's achievements to have appreciated what Arsenal Football Club means in its entirety to supporters who followed the team long before his own arrival at the club.

Wenger has instinctively understood the high expectations naturally held by the Arsenal fan. In his early days at the club, he was also quick to appreciate the age-old rivalry between Arsenal and their local rivals Tottenham Hotspur. Most of all, Wenger seemed to understand the spirit of Arsenal that exists for far more than just ninety minutes on a Saturday afternoon.

Perhaps this is one of Wenger's less-heralded achievements: to have realised, from the start, that he is part of something bigger through his work at Arsenal Football Club and, through that work, to make Arsenal Football Club even bigger still.

'The life of a club never stops.'

22 September 1996 – that first press conference again.

'Arsenal fans are intelligent. They know how to judge someone on his work and ideas, not just his reputation.'

September 1996 – immediately prior to taking charge of the Arsenal team.

'Today ... Arsenal was Arsenal, with the fighting spirit.'

1 February 1997 – after a hard-fought but goalless game with Leeds.

'I went to Barcelona with Monaco and there were 120,000 people there. Yet it was almost quiet compared with our game against Spurs at Highbury.'

14 February 1997.

'If spirit won prizes, Arsenal would win the lot.'

17 March 1998 – after beating West Ham on penalties to reach the FA Cup semi-final.

'Arsenal's history is important. At some clubs success is accidental; at Arsenal it is compulsory.'

29 April 1998 – *en route* to making his own history as only the second Arsenal manager to win the Double.

'I realised after three or four games here that I was at a big club.'

15 May 1998.

'We are strong at home, and that's always the basis of a good season.'

26 December 2000.

'I am aware of the rivalry.'

23 November 1996 – prior to Wenger's first derby game against Tottenham.

'I cannot see Spurs doing us a favour at Old Trafford on Sunday.'

11 May 1999 – after defeat by Leeds leaves Arsenal needing help from their local rivals if they are to retain the Premiership title. They didn't get it.

'The fans create an atmosphere in which you feel you have to go for it.'

6 November 1999 – prior to another derby at White Hart Lane in which Spurs would record a rare victory over a Wenger team.

'I accept rivalry and competition but I cannot accept a player's choice should be based on what a few overexcited people feel about the club.'

4 July 2001 – after the signing of Sol Campbell from Tottenham, a move that angered many Spurs fans to the point where they hung an effigy of Campbell outside White Hart Lane.

'What's important is to win the title. It doesn't matter where it is.'

17 April 2004 – when faced with the likelihood of Arsenal winning the title at Tottenham's home ground.

'Whatever happens we won't be provocative.'

23 April 2004 – looking forward to sealing the title at White Hart Lane.

'It must have been good for the fans to see us repeat what happened in 1971 when we also won the title at Tottenham.'

25 April 2004 – after the title is secured, and Wenger reveals his own knowledge of Arsenal history.

'Derby games are either completely locked or completely crazy. Today we got the crazy version.'

13 November 2004 – Tottenham Hotspur 4 Arsenal 5.

'My assistant is Pat Rice and without him I would have made many mistakes; he knows the spirit of the club and how English players react. Somebody who has the feelings for the club can react properly and respond on behalf of the local people. It is very, very important.'

3 April 1998 – in praise of a lifelong servant of Arsenal Football Club, assistant manager Pat Rice, a member of the 1971 Double-winning side.

'He [Boro Primorac] has worked with me for a long time and I rate his contribution highly. But it is always difficult to say exactly how important someone is. He is like Pat Rice in that he works hard with me every day and he contributes highly on the pitch. He's a good football technician and he knows what I want.'

28 March 2004 – Wenger praises his first-team coach Boro Primorac, a back-room figure with a key technical role in Arsenal's successes ...

'When you come out at Bolton on Tuesday and see all your fans there, you know they have had to take the bus after working all day; they have to travel back and be up early for work again ... where else can you get that?'

... and still more praise, this time for the travelling Arsenal faithful.

'We send scouts where others don't look.'

3 August 2000 – after the signing of unknown Lithuanian Tomas Danilevicius from the Swiss side Lausanne.

'The most important thing for me is that our club is healthy.'

3 August 2000 – defending Arsenal's prudent dealings in the transfer market.

'It is the fans who make our game, not the managers, the clubs or the players.'

1 September 2000 – and more on the lifeblood of football.

'The fans have always been loyal to me since I've been here.'

6 December 2001.

'I believe the ambition of the club must be so strong and the feeling of the players so strong that I do not have to force players to stay.'

23 December 2001.

'A team is not only about buying players but growing together and slowly building belief, confidence and the connections in the team. I think we are slowly getting there.'

17 September 2002.

'This club has such an illustrious past, but today is one of the most important dates in our history.'

23 February 2004 – the day Arsenal announced the final go-ahead for their new 60,000-capacity stadium at Ashburton Grove.

'It's a 100 per cent supportive atmosphere, and that's why I'm still here. That's what makes the club special, as there's a trust you don't find in many places.'

14 April 2004 – explaining his continuing presence at Arsenal Football Club, an old institution founded on old-fashioned values?

Ferguson

Traditionally, Arsenal's greatest rivals have been their neighbours, Tottenham Hotspur. But the Wenger era has coincided with a long period of underachievement at Spurs, when Arsenal have fought their most bitter battles with Manchester United and Arsène Wenger's most bitter rival has been his United counterpart, Sir Alex Ferguson.

So enduring and so personal has this contest become that newspapers have called on psychologists to examine the personality contrasts between the cerebral, professional-class Frenchman and the passionate, working-class Scotsman. Whatever the psychology, the battle between Wenger and Ferguson has been played out on the football field in a succession of epic encounters between their teams. But it is the battle of managerial wills off the field that has proved, if anything, even more engaging.

It was in 1997 that the first outbreak of 'mind games' between Wenger and Ferguson was reported, and the years since have seen both men resort to media comment in pursuit of advantage. Well into the new century, an English football season did not seem complete without a war of words between Alex Ferguson and Arsène Wenger and, by 2005, the rivalry between the two men showed no sign of mellowing.

'We both want to win and neither of us hides from having a go at each other.'

5 May 2002 – this Wenger comment about his relationship with Sir Alex Ferguson could apply to any date from 1996 onwards.

'I was surprised to see Ferguson on the pitch because you can only play eleven.'

19 February 1997 – after Arsenal lose to Manchester United at Highbury. The game was marred by an unsavoury clash between Arsenal's Ian Wright and United's goalkeeper Peter Schmeichel, an incident that prompted the United manager to run on to the pitch in protest.

'It's wrong the programme is extended so Manchester United can rest and win everything.'

3 April 1997 – in response to the Ferguson-touted possibility that the Old Trafford team might be granted more time to complete their Premiership programme of matches.

'This is the right decision for this season. It is impossible to change the rules so near to the end of the competition.'

11 April 1997 – Manchester United are ordered to fulfil their fixtures as scheduled, and Wenger wins his first off-field battle with Ferguson.

'He doesn't bother me. Perhaps the more sensitive can be affected. I understand his passion and if I get under his skin then that is good.'

November 1997.

'What he [Ferguson] said does not bother me at all and I do not want to make a fuss about it. I think it was just a little bit clumsy on his part.'

4 January 1999 – in response to quoted remarks by Alex Ferguson that described Arsenal as a 'belligerent' team who liked a 'scrap'. Ferguson subsequently claimed to have been misquoted and announced that he had written a letter of apology to the Arsenal manager.

'If he has written the letter then it must have been sent by horse because I haven't received it.'

8 January 1999 – nothing from Manchester in the post.

'I give a slight advantage to Chelsea.'

1 March 1999 – when asked if Manchester United or Chelsea were Arsenal's main rivals in the Premiership run-in ...

'The Champions Cup is special in everybody's mind – and I would say even more so in United's mind – so I think they might lose more energy.'

... citing Manchester United's European commitments as the reason.

'You have to say he [Ferguson] did not win things for a long time at Old Trafford. When you think about managers today, they only get five or six months to be successful whereas Alex got five or six years.'

10 April 1999 – reflecting on his rival's early and trophy-free years at Manchester United ...

'I think the word is respect. I can't say there is friendship on both sides.'

... and responding to Ferguson's claim that he was on friendly terms with his Arsenal counterpart.

'He is not stupid and I am not.'

1 October 2000 – prior to another showdown with United at Highbury ...

'The managers will not be playing at 4pm today, although I'd like it if he [Ferguson] played. Maybe we could play one against one after the game.'

... and Wenger offers single combat with his greatest rival.

'Ferguson feels Chelsea are the team to beat – are they the biggest threat? I don't feel that.'

9 August 2001 – in response to the United manager's comment that he considered Chelsea to be his team's likely principal rival in the season ahead.

'I don't agree with Ferguson.'

24 October 2001 – in response to the suggestion that United's Ruud van Nistelrooy was a better striker than Arsenal's Thierry Henry.

'I think it will be very difficult for him [Ferguson] to stop, because it's an addiction when you stay in the game for such a long time. Just imagine the same guy sitting at home Saturday afternoon at three o'clock and asking himself, "What's happening to me? It looks so different."'

1 October 2000 – on Ferguson's apparently final decision to retire at the age of 60 at the end of the 2001–02 season.

'Alex Ferguson has a strong voice and he cares for the game.'

25 February 2001 – Wenger praises his United counterpart. This requires some explanation. At the time, proposals were circulating which would allow players to transfer between clubs more or less at will. Wenger opposed this idea vociferously and now urged Ferguson to use his personal authority to do the same.

'Alex has done marvellously well, but his club has such potential they will continue to be tough, no matter who comes in after him. It will not be a relief when he retires. They have the money to buy a good manager, the money to buy good players. It will go on. United have twice our budget, but I don't envy that because, frankly, I enjoy our rivalry.'

23 November 2001 – on his greatest rival, who at that time was still scheduled to retire at the end of the season ...

'When we meet sometimes – at airports or UEFA meetings, things like that – we don't hit each other. In fact, it's sometimes quite funny when we meet.'

... and whose relationship with Wenger could have its lighter side, at least according to the Arsenal manager.

'I'm pleased he's staying on. I'm pleased because I know now who I must fight. It's something I like because I know I'll face a tough Manchester United in the next few years and they will want to get even stronger. I'd miss the rivalry, too. Our mind games keep me on my toes.'

February 2002 – after Ferguson decides not to retire after all.

'His [Ferguson's] only weakness is that he thinks he doesn't have one.'

March 2002 – fuelling an increasingly hostile war of words in the closing stages of the 2001–02 campaign.

'We are confident, not stupid. I respect Alex but I am ignoring his comments in the same way I ignore all comments about Arsenal.'

26 April 2002 – swatting away Ferguson's suggestion that over-confidence was Arsenal's weakness, as Wenger's team closed in on the Premiership title.

'Everyone thinks they have the prettiest wife at home.'

2 May 2002 – Arsène Wenger's most famous comment, in response to Ferguson's suggestion that, despite being in second place behind Arsenal, his team 'played the best football in England'.

'I don't know what Alex Ferguson really means.'

4 May 2002 – after Arsenal's FA Cup Final victory over Chelsea, when Sir Alex Ferguson had once again claimed that United were the best team in England.

'What are all these asterisks in the newspaper?'

8 May 2002 – fine fooling prior to the game at Old Trafford, where Arsenal needed just a point to secure the Premiership title. The newspaper concerned was one of many 8 May 2002 editions that described an Alex Ferguson press conference, where journalists had suggested to the United boss that his £28 million purchase of Juan Sebastian Veron was a waste of money. Ferguson stormed out, leaving reporters with a volley of obscenities, which were then reported, suitably asterisked.

'I don't know if Alex Ferguson is rattled or will congratulate us if we do it, but the table doesn't lie. It's always right.'

8 May 2002.

'Winning the title at Old Trafford will have no special significance.'

8 May 2002 – another pre-match comment. Few believed him.

'I would like to have signed Rio Ferdinand, but for £10 million less.'

July 2002 – giving his opinion on another expensive Manchester United purchase.

'It's not a poker game.'

10 December 2002 – on his all-in rivalry with Ferguson.

'I have no gift for paranoia.'

2003 – another springtime, another title chase with United and another war of words, as Wenger describes one gift that he did not possess, though with the clear insinuation that such a gift was possessed by others, maybe even Sir Alex ...

'I would not agree with Sir Alex. I would not say we have been triumphalist. We are confident, and there is a big difference.'

... as the accusation of triumphalism levelled by Ferguson at Arsenal is given short shrift by Arsène Wenger ...

'I prefer wine to whisky.'

... and Wenger states his own reasons for never taking an after-match drink at Old Trafford.

'I don't hate anybody. I am not thinking about Alex Ferguson.'

16 April 2003 – during the build-up to the title showdown game with United.

'I don't know whether he [Ferguson] likes me or not. I don't know him well enough and these things don't worry me.'

A self-explanatory opinion from the Arsenal boss.

'One of the things that made Manchester great is going.'

20 June 2003 – Wenger offers his view on David Beckham's £25 million move to Real Madrid ...

'The personal problems between Beckham and Ferguson certainly lowered the fee.'

... and still more public comment to follow on a matter of no direct interest whatsoever to Arsenal Football Club.

'If you want to see Martin Keown as a devil and van Nistelrooy as an angel then you have a big problem because van Nistelrooy is quite provocative and every Arsenal player knows that.'

22 September 2003 – after a 0–0 draw at Old Trafford notable for many episodes of dubious nature. These included a ferocious taunting of Manchester United's striker by Arsenal's veteran defender after van Nistelrooy had missed a last-minute penalty. The encounter would soon be known as the Battle of Old Trafford.

'It has been too quiet between us this season ... we locked horns before because we were both challenging for the title. This season we've been in front virtually from the start so there has been no point.'

2 May 2004 – as the alpha male, at least for the season.

'I think he [Ferguson] has a good sense of humour, you can't deny that, and maybe it would be better if you put us up against a wall and shot us all.'

19 October 2004 – after Ferguson offers his opinion that Arsenal were punished too lightly for their behaviour in the previous season's fixture. Wenger responds from the lofty position of League-leading champions, then on a run of 49 games unbeaten ...

'I hope that he will calm down.'

... and offers some medical advice to his great rival.

'I don't think there is another rivalry in English football like the one between him and me. It is special. We get on OK. When we meet, it is in situations of immense tension, immense happiness or disappointment. Away from games, we have had interesting conversations about football. There is no bitterness.'

22 October 2004 – reflective words in advance of another Wenger-Ferguson showdown at Old Trafford, a fiery encounter which would soon become known as the Battle of the Buffet.

'I will never answer any questions any more about this man ... He doesn't interest me and doesn't matter to me at all ... I will never answer to any provocation from him any more.'

15 January 2005 – surely some bitterness almost three months on from the Battle of the Buffet. With another Arsenal-United game imminent, Ferguson chooses to impugn the character of Arsenal FC and its manager, using events of October 2004 as cover. Wenger's furious response comes on a Saturday evening, right after his team have suffered a horrible Premiership defeat at Bolton ...

'I have no diplomatic relations with him.'

... and Wenger loses his cool along with the three points.

'He [Ferguson] has pushed the cork in a bit far this time.'

17 January 2005 – and Wenger's vow of silence lasts for less than 48 hours, as Ferguson's comments clearly rattle the Arsenal boss.

Prophesy

Professional football is a human activity with a strong emotional quality and, during the summer of 2002, Arsenal fans were as overjoyed as they had ever been. Their team had broken Manchester United's three-year stranglehold on the Premiership, and Arsène Wenger had talked openly of a lasting shift in the balance of football power, in favour of his own exciting team.

When the 2002–03 season began, it was not only Arsenal supporters who appreciated the efforts of Arsène Wenger's players. In the early weeks of that season, Arsenal continued a domestic unbeaten run that dated back to Christmas 2001, winning game after game with dream football perhaps never seen before in the English game.

At this juncture, Arsène Wenger allowed himself to think publicly about what his team was capable of achieving, in a series of widely reported comments. These suggested to many that even cerebral Frenchmen could allow their emotions to rule their reason.

'It would not surprise me if we went unbeaten all season.'

18 August 2002.

'It's not impossible to go through the season unbeaten and I can't see why it's shocking to say that. Every manager thinks that but they don't say it because they're scared it would be ridiculous.'

20 September 2002 – the day before a Premiership game at Bolton.

'If we have the right attitude, we can go through the season unbeaten. I'm not tempting fate by saying what I believe.'

21 September 2002 – after victory at Bolton which was Arsenal's 28th consecutive Premiership game without defeat ...

'It was done by Milan in 1992. I can't see why it's so shocking to say that we can do it this season. If we lose, people will turn and say, "You have a big mouth," but I can only be honest. If I say I have no confidence in a team that's gone 28 games unbeaten you'd call me a liar. It's everyone's dream to go through a season without losing, so let's give it our best shot. If it doesn't happen it's not the end of the world.'

... giving Wenger the chance to put his vision into some kind of context.

'I am still hopeful we can go through the season unbeaten – a frightening thought.'

28 September 2002.

Lamentations 2

Wenger's 2002 comments about going through a Premiership season unbeaten were met with howls of ridicule from football commentators. They 'knew', it was a 'fact' that, no matter how great a team was, the feat of playing 38 matches in a season without losing was, quite simply, impossible.

Within days, these voices of scorn appeared wholly vindicated as Wenger's previously invincible team lost a game, then another, and another, and another, as the gods of football seemed to punish the Arsenal manager for his presumption. Two of these defeats came in Europe, where success continued to prove out of reach for Arsène Wenger's players.

Despite this, the spring of 2003 saw Arsenal back on top of the domestic league, and odds-on to achieve the unheard-of feat of back-to-back Doubles. But Wenger's great rival Sir Alex Ferguson had other ideas, and it was Manchester United who emerged victorious from a heated Premiership run-in, both on and off the field.

Arsenal therefore ended the 2002–03 season with 'only' the FA Cup to show for their efforts and, although Manchester United's achievement in regaining the Premiership was considerable, it was widely felt that Arsenal had 'thrown away' their title. Perhaps Wenger himself shared this view as, for once, he appeared to lose something of his *sang-froid*, as the reality of second place dawned once more upon him.

'We were beaten by a special goal from a very special talent … he is the biggest talent I have seen since I arrived in England.'

19 October 2002 – after a wonder goal from Everton's sixteen-year-old Wayne Rooney ends Arsenal's unbeaten Premiership run after 30 games.

'We have not come to a full stop. Maybe we have taken our foot off the accelerator slightly. That's all. It's not like a car that has hit a tree at 160mph.'

21 October 2002 – Wenger suggests that one defeat hardly constitutes a crash.

'There is no reason to be alarmist. You have periods like these in a season.'

22 October 2002 – after Arsenal's Champions League defeat by Auxerre.

'You felt they had an angel behind their goalkeeper.'

26 October 2002 – Blackburn goalie Brad Friedel is apparently divinely assisted as his team inflict a third straight defeat on Arsenal.

'The referee made a difference. All credit to him, he scored a good second goal for them. I was happy for him. He deserves a good mention.'

30 October 2002 – sarcasm after Borussia Dortmund beat Arsenal 2–1 with the aid of a disputed penalty.

'Ten days before our first defeat, we were the best team in the country so I don't believe that ten days later we can be the worst.'

3 November 2002 – prior to a Premiership game against Fulham, and the Arsenal manager appeals for a sense of perspective after four straight losses.

'If you lose four you have to be concerned. We're not used to losing runs.'

3 November 2002 – after winning ways are restored.

'We are very disappointed.'

19 March 2003 – another Champions League campaign ends before the knockout stages following a 2–1 defeat in Valencia.

'We can complain and cry the whole night but that will not change the result.'

17 September 2003 – Arsenal 0 Inter Milan 3.

'Don't forget we got the UEFA Fair Play Award. If you want to be objective, you have to mention that. It's the only European trophy we have won!'

26 September 2003 – an appeal for balanced reporting in the aftermath of the 'Battle of Old Trafford'.

'Football is cruel. It's like that – difficult to accept.'

6 February 2004 – Arsenal go out of the Champions League again, beaten at home by Chelsea in the quarter-final, days after losing an FA Cup semi-final to Manchester United.

'United were more aggressive and committed and they wanted it more.'

7 December 2002 – Manchester United beat Arsenal 2–0, bringing to an end a run of 55 Premiership games in which Arsenal had scored at least one goal.

'We lost concentration for a minute and the title race is still wide open. I would not say anyone is in the driving seat. We go from game to game and things can happen so quickly but we have a very good chance.'

16 April 2003 – after a 2–2 draw with Manchester United which was widely felt to be a better result for United than for Arsenal.

'I don't know what went wrong.'

26 April 2003 – after a 2–2 draw with Bolton, which was even more widely felt to be a better result for United than for Arsenal.

'It's not in our hands any more – that's the most disappointing thing.'

... further reflections on the implication of the Bolton game.

'I have dropped every bit of blood and energy to fight for first place. I would be the proudest man in the world if we had won.'

4 May 2003 – a loss to Leeds confirms Manchester United's recapture of the Premiership title ...

LAMENTATIONS 2

'I am deeply disappointed – do you think I fight the whole season to finish second?'

... as Arsenal do exactly that for the fourth time in five years ...

'Are United worthy? I don't know.'

... and the wine-loving Wenger partakes of a somewhat sour grape.

'I am not a great writer.'

May 2003 – Wenger is still sniffy in response to suggestions that he write to Sir Alex Ferguson to congratulate him on his team's Premiership title, as Ferguson had so written to Wenger the previous year ...

'I still think if you look at the championship and the FA Cup we are certainly the best team.'

... and all of a sudden the League table isn't quite as all-revealing as previously suggested.

'I hope we can find a magician.'

5 May 2003 – when asked how Arsenal might close the financial gap between themselves and Manchester United.

'I hope that, for the next twenty years, we will have seasons as disappointing as this one.'

17 May 2003 – a perhaps rueful touch of humour after victory over Southampton in Cardiff leaves Arsenal with 'only' the FA Cup to show for their season's efforts …

'We finished runners-up [in the Premiership] and won the FA Cup and were very close to a double Double. Considering the opposition, that's not bad.'

… prompting Wenger to place his team's season in some sort of context.

Cups

Arsenal's 2003 FA Cup triumph was widely portrayed as a 'consolation' prize, after the loss of the Premiership to Manchester United. This reflected the huge achievements now expected of Arsenal as a matter of course, a level of expectation which Arsène Wenger's own comments had done much to generate.

But for all the Premiership disappointment, it was hard to sniff at three Cup victories in six years, and Arsène Wenger has always understood the special position held by the FA Cup within the English game. Indeed, some of his comments on the tournament have suggested a Frenchman's love of the FA Cup as deep as that of any Englishman. There can be no doubt that Wenger has maintained the utmost respect for the oldest of all football competitions, at a time when others were, perhaps, less respectful.

But Wenger's views on the FA Cup and other cup competitions have always been entirely his own, and the busy match schedule endured by successful modern teams has often been the cause of these comments. From his earliest years at Arsenal, he has been especially keen to suggest that there are some cup games his team can do without.

'It is far more difficult to finish sixth in the league than to win the Worthington Cup.'

22 February 2002 – a rare comment on the League Cup, the so-called 'second best cup competition in England', which Wenger has consistently treated as such, regardless of its sponsors.

'For me the most important thing is the championship. So every time we play one more game it reduces our chances to be fresh in championship games. So I cannot be happy. But, on the other hand, in the quarter-final of the FA Cup you cannot calculate – you have to give everything to go through.'

8 March 1998 – following the 1–1 FA Cup draw with West Ham that meant the apparently tedious necessity of a replay.

'The FA Cup is special all over the world, because of the tradition.'

3 April 1998 – prior to an English FA Cup semi-final with Wolves ...

'I experienced three semi-finals with Monaco, losing two and winning one, so I know from experience how difficult it is to get through a semi-final. It's like crossing the road. You have to look left then right before you get to the other side.'

... prompting some uniquely continental observations.

'He [Kanu] hadn't seen the injured player at the other end. He didn't realise the keeper had kicked it out deliberately.'

13 February 1999 – some fun and games at Highbury, after Arsenal had 'beaten' Sheffield United 2–1 in an FA Cup fifth-round tie. Arsenal's winner was controversial, to say the least, when Ray Parlour took a throw-in, intending to return the ball to Sheffield United, who had kicked the ball out of play following an injury to one of their players. Unfortunately, Arsenal's newly signed Nigerian striker Kanu appeared not to appreciate the throw-in-after-injury convention. To the astonishment of Sheffield United and of most of the crowd, Kanu intercepted the ball and passed to Marc Overmars, who scored. Under the rules of the game, the 'goal' had to stand, in the face of huge protests from Sheffield that seemed certain to continue long after the final whistle, until Wenger began his post-match comments by explaining Kanu's misunderstanding ...

'Kanu is feeling very down. He's very sad. It was an accident.'

... sympathetically understood by Wenger, who immediately offered to replay the game, an offer accepted in good spirit by Sheffield manager Steve Bruce ...

'We didn't want to cheat.'

... leaving the Arsenal manager somewhere near the moral high ground, to the surprise of many ...

'We have a fair spirit, but we're not stupid.'

... but still insistent that the replayed game would be played at Highbury.

'We've won the game but now we can lose again.'

23 February 1999 – in advance of the replayed game with Sheffield. Despite Wenger's thoughts of doom, Arsenal duly won the match by an identical 2–1 scoreline.

'It was just not our night.'

14 April 1999 – as Arsenal fail to get to the other side of an epic semi-final replay with Manchester United notable for an amazing winner by United's Ryan Giggs ...

'We were a little bit unlucky, lost the ball in the middle of the park and Giggs did the rest.'

... and all of a sudden Wenger sounds as sick as a parrot.

'There was one turning point when Giggs had his chance at 0–0.'

15 February 2003 – four years on, and some kind of reckoning for Ryan Giggs after a 2–0 FA Cup victory over Manchester United in which United's Welsh winger failed to tap the ball into an open goal early in the game ...

'Of course he [Giggs] should have scored in that situation, but everyone misses sometimes.'

... prompting an almost sympathetic response from a grateful Wenger.

'I think it's unfair and a bad decision. The FA Cup is something that has worldwide fame and the fact that such a prestigious club as Manchester United are out of the competition is just untrue. It's not normal.'

9 July 1999 – Wenger reacts furiously to the news that the FA Cup holders Manchester United would not defend their trophy in the 1999–2000 season, but would instead travel to Brazil to take part in a newly created World Club Championship ...

'It could also give United an advantage in the League.'

... and it's not only the prestige of the FA Cup that might be affected by United's decision.

'I'm a non-admirer of the decision made at the start of the season to allow them [Manchester United] to get out of the FA Cup.'

23 January 2000 – augustly reiterating his views on United's withdrawal.

'Yellow cards given in semi-finals should go into the next season.'

19 April 2000 – in advance of the UEFA Cup semi-final second leg at Lens. Eight members of Arsenal's squad were on a yellow card, and one booking away from missing the final, if they qualified. In the end, Arsenal secured their final place without incurring any suspensions, and no more was heard of Wenger's suggestion.

'I would rather finish the tie on the day, going to extra-time and then penalties if need be, from the third round onwards.'

10 March 2003 – after another FA Cup replay is needed after a 2–2 draw with Chelsea, and Wenger returns to ideas for reform. Arsenal won the replay without the need for penalties and went on to win that year's competition.

'I would advocate playing all FA Cup ties on a Wednesday.'

11 May 2001 – and more proposed reforms.

'We play from August to May because before football was amateur and you had the holiday in the summers. But now we are professional people. We don't play football in the best period of the season which is May, June and July.'

13 December 2002 – advocating a change in the football calendar.

'[The FA Cup Final is] a special day for everybody, because it is still the biggest event in the world on the day. Look at the number of countries that take the FA Cup Final on television. I don't know exactly how many it is, but it will be a crazy number. So I think it still has a huge impact. I remember I was in Thailand when Manchester United played Newcastle in the final three years ago and it was live there on normal TV.'

27 April 2002.

'We will be up for it and will give every drop of blood.'

25 March 2003 – explaining how Arsenal intended to win their Cup quarter-final replay against Chelsea.

'We have always shown total respect for the FA Cup.'

11 April 2003 – and surely not suggesting that others hadn't?

'It would be terrible to go out of the FA Cup.'

18 January 2000 – the day before an FA Cup fourth-round replay with Leicester City. Arsenal would lose on penalties.

'There is an atmosphere about the FA Cup that cannot be ignored and which makes it still a magical competition.'

5 April 2001.

'People say losing in the final is a disaster and of course it's bad, but first you have to get to the final. I have got there twice and we treat the FA Cup Final as something very important.'

25 January 2002.

'When you don't qualify everyone is responsible, the managers, the players and the coaching staff; we are all in the same boat.'

20 March 2003 – after Arsenal's hopes of a Champions League semi-final are sunk by Valencia.

'Today, at a club like Arsenal, the UEFA Cup is not enough to give you a complete season.'

13 May 2000.

'We have a 50–50 chance. And we just have to go for it. In a cup final you just try to win it.'

17 May 2000 – in Copenhagen, prior to the UEFA Cup Final against Galatasaray. Arsenal lost on penalties.

'What is amazing is that we are in a situation that we can lose the game next week and go through, or win it and go out. It makes it a little bit strange and it would be very difficult to explain even to a mathematician.'

12 March 2002 – as Arsenal look forward to the final game of a far from settled Champions League group.

CUPS

'When I was growing up, the [FA Cup] Final was the only overseas football I could see. It was huge, something from a different planet.'

11 May 2003 – in advance of his fourth FA Cup Final with Arsenal, and Wenger recalls the importance of the competition in his own boyhood in Alsace ...

'There was only one TV in our village. It was in the school. And, although you had to pay to get in, you still had to be there early for a seat. I was maybe nine or ten at the time.'

... a different world entirely from that which faced him in 2003 ...

'I don't need to pay to get in at Cardiff – I'm paid to go there.'

... in more ways than one.

'The fans respond strongly to the FA Cup and the biggest disappointment for them since I've been here was losing the [2001] final to Liverpool.'

2 January 2004 – another FA Cup campaign looms, and Wenger hints at the importance of the competition to the Arsenal supporters.

'We really have to win.'

25 November 2003 – prior to another Champions League game in Milan which Arsenal had to, er, win, to avoid another early exit.

'Not in my wildest dreams could we have predicted that sort of result.'

25 November 2003 – Inter Milan 1 Arsenal 5, and perhaps, at last, Arsenal begin to lay down a European reputation.

'The result is wonderful. But it is even more enjoyable to see opposition fans cheering our team.'

6 March 2004 – Arsenal turn on the style in an another awe-inspiring 5–1 victory, this time in a FA Cup quarter-final at Portsmouth, whose supporters appreciated fully the quality of the football played by Wenger's team.

'We wanted to go for everything and that's where maybe I made a mistake. I should have dropped the FA Cup earlier.'

3 May 2004 – a rueful reflection on Arsenal's 2004 pursuit of glory on three fronts.

'The team that wins the European Cup is not necessarily the best team in Europe; the team that wins the FA Cup is not necessarily the best team in the country.'

9 April 2004 – for all the romance of the cups, it's league competition that matters most to Arsène Wenger.

Gunners 2

In the course of his years as manager of Arsenal, Arsène Wenger has transformed a largely English team into a largely foreign team. As the English old guard moved into well-earned retirement, their places were taken by new signings such as Kolo Touré and Lauren, previously-unheralded players whose potential was spotted by Wenger's global scouting network. But it was only under Wenger's coaching that players like these fulfilled their potential and became consistent players of international class.

By 2003, Arsène Wenger had created a talented squad whose members hailed from Africa, South America and continental Europe, with certain Englishmen still deployed in key positions on the field. But, whatever their nationality, Arsenal players could expect to be praised in equal measure in their manager's public statements.

But even this most team-minded of managers could also appreciate that there were certain players who could be more equal than others on the football field. From 1999 onwards, Arsène Wenger found himself called upon time and again to comment on the gifts of one Arsenal player in particular, a striker from his own homeland especially blessed with the gift of 'va va voom'.

'He is quite a good finisher.'

21 August 1999 – perhaps understating the talents of the recently signed Frenchman Thierry Henry.

'He is a very welcome addition to our squad and will be a great asset to us as he has already proved his talent at club and international level.'

15 January 1999 – accurately stating the talents of the recently signed Nigerian Kanu.

'He is an experienced international and a very competent defender who will prove to be a great asset to the club.'

5 September 2000 – maybe overstating the talents of the recently signed Latvian Igors Stepanovs.

'All his goals are best-sellers.'

26 April 1998 – on big-at-the-box-office Bergkamp.

'If he (Bergkamp) gives the impression of being laid-back, he isn't. He works hard. What I like in his game is he makes complicated situations look very simple.'

23 April 1999.

'He's a player who gets close to perfection.'

2 March 2002 – after Bergkamp's scarcely credible goal of the season at Newcastle.

'We saw the real Sol Campbell … it is good for England to see him playing so well under tremendous pressure.'

17 November 2001 – and Wenger's recently signed defender makes his first return to Tottenham as an Arsenal player, where he turns in an immense performance in the face of 'Judas' cries from the home fans.

'You tend to see the best of him when you need someone to be a hero.'

More praise for Campbell during the run-in to the 2002 title.

'Sol is an absolute lion for us.'

1 October 2002.

'This week, Patrick still plays for us.'

**22 January 2002 – in response to rumours that Patrick Vieira
was planning to join Real Madrid in the summer of 2002,
rumours that further suggested that Wenger had struck an
unofficial agreement with his player to facilitate the move ...**

'That just shows the imagination of the English people is
still great, which is quite positive for the nation ... there is
no agreement between us.'

... prompting a further denial from Wenger.

'Patrick [Vieira] is an animal – just speak to the players
who play against him.'

15 August 2004 – on a big beast of the Premiership jungle.

'He is a versatile player, comfortable in both defence and midfield. He possesses strong, physical power as well as great stamina.'

30 May 2000 – on signing Cameroon international Lauren.

'I still think we have got two great players in Lauren and Pires.'

18 August 2000 – after Frenchman Robert Pires had also moved to Highbury.

'It's simple really. If Wiltord behaves like everybody else there is no problem.'

21 December 2001 – on rumours that Sylvain Wiltord was unhappy at Arsenal.

'Both [Ray] Parlour and [Freddie] Ljungberg were absolutely fantastic today.'

4 May 2002 – praise for Arsenal's two goalscorers in their FA Cup Final victory over Chelsea.

'Kanu and Bergkamp together doesn't work. We have tried it, but I've come to the conclusion that it's not an ideal pair.'

17 December 2000.

'Ashley is a strong character and one of his strengths is that, no matter who he plays, or where he plays, he plays his game.'

23 August 2002 – explaining the talents of Ashley Cole, Arsenal football player.

'It was a difficult game for Kanu but he turned the fans around and by the end they were chanting his name.'

23 September 2002 – praise for Arsenal's Nigerian striker after a poor first-half against Bolton is followed by a injury-time winner.

'The two Brazilians will have a big effect on the team because they are at its heart in the middle of the park. I'm very happy to have them here because they are two outstanding characters and two team players.'

17 August 2002 – on Gilberto Silva and Edu.

'I didn't expect him to score so many goals but when you buy players you sometimes get pleasant surprises.'

2 October 2002 – on Gilberto's goal-scoring talents.

'We have a game based on movement, technique and pace and he has all of that.'

27 January 2004 – commenting on the signing of José Antonio Reyes.

'I don't look at the passport of people but at the quality and attitude.'

14 February 2005 – after a game against Crystal Palace for which Wenger selected a starting eleven and five substitutes who were all from overseas, the first time this had ever happened in the Premiership. Arsenal won 5–1.

'He has pace and dribbling power and makes things happen. He has a good spirit and mentality and a good experience at international level.'

3 August 1999 – the day Arsenal announced the signing of Thierry Henry.

'Henry has so much more power. He is a boxer with such a strong build. It's difficult for any defender to fight against him.'

6 May 2000 – after two goals from Henry secured a 2–1 win over Chelsea.

'You could say that we all play for him, in a way.'

October 2002 – succinctly expressing Henry's importance to the Arsenal team.

'I have known Thierry since he was seventeen at Monaco, but every season since he's been at Arsenal he has improved and this year he has done so much more than ever before.'

2 October 2002.

'He [Henry] makes the pitch look small when he has the ball.'

16 November 2002.

'He is a fantastic striker – the exception becomes the norm with him.'

12 January 2003 – after two goals from Henry secured a 4–0 victory at Birmingham.

'Should we lose a player like Thierry Henry, then I would say, "Yes, we are in desperate situation."'

24 October 2003 – an indisputable estimation of Henry's value to Arsenal.

'Thierry is amazing. A dream you want as a player. He says, "Give me the ball and I can pass you because I have the acceleration to do that." It must be an amazing feeling to be able to do that. Such power.'

14 December 2003 – some time after Henry began to appear in car commercials with the catchphrase 'va-va-voom', as his club manager may have appreciated, if only subconsciously …

'Sometimes you say that God has not given you everything, but with Thierry he has been given a lot.'

… prompting talk of spiritual forces from a grateful earthly manager.

'When Henry gets the ball anywhere he can be in the opposition's box in a fraction of a second.'

30 August 2004.

'He dedicates his free time to recovery, does everything right. He doesn't drink, doesn't go out – you can call him any night at ten o'clock and he's at home.'

4 October 2004 – in praise of Henry's off-field activities, or lack of them.

'I can only guarantee one thing with this team, and that is they will give everything to win each game.'

9 April 2004 – and a reminder of football's being a team game.

'We have a team constructed to be offensive.'

13 November 2004 – as opposed to 'defensive'.

Discipline 2

By 2003, there could be no doubting the offensive firepower of Arsène Wenger's Arsenal team. But his players also retained the capacity to cause offence in the matter of on-field misconduct. In his early years at Highbury, Arsène Wenger established a reputation for publicly supporting his players in all matters relating to on-field discipline. The reputation remained well earned in the years that followed, with Patrick Vieira continuing to receive regular public support from his manager.

Many commentators argued that Wenger's apparently blind support for all his players was a dubious and wholly deliberate strategy intended to foster team spirit, and it has to be said that Arsenal's successes in the early 2000s were notable for a powerful sense of team unity. But Wenger's strategy has also compelled this most hands-on of football coaches to spend a huge amount of time engaged in ongoing disciplinary sagas, examples of which have involved not only Patrick Vieira but also Arsène Wenger himself.

Seven years into his period at Highbury, Wenger could bring himself to joke about Arsenal's disciplinary record, which often appeared to interest the media more than Arsenal's football. But nothing could prepare him for the media frenzy that followed one particular Arsenal game in September 2003 – a fiery encounter with Manchester United that would enter football legend as the Battle of Old Trafford.

'Patrick [Vieira] has tried to play football, and some others have not. In the end he is sent off for a bad reaction. It's unbelievable.'

19 August 2000 – in some fury, after an opening-day defeat at Sunderland that brought trouble for the Arsenal player and, though he did not know it at the time, the Arsenal manager.

'The ref is human: he makes mistakes sometimes but at the end of the day Patrick took a red card again.'

21 August 2000 – after Vieira's second dismissal in three days against Liverpool.

'I don't think he [Vieira] will leave. He is very down and frustrated but he wants to stay because he loves the club.'

23 August 2000 – commenting on reports that Vieira had hinted at quitting English football, fed up with being sent off so often. Later that day, his manager found himself with his own disciplinary matters to attend to, as he was charged with 'alleged threatening behaviour and physical intimidation' during an encounter with a match official after the Sunderland game four days previously.

'I'm pleased that we could win this game after such a controversial week, and as well by the performance of Patrick Vieira today. Because he was outstanding and exceptional ... Never for a minute did I think of not playing him. Because I know how strong this guy is mentally. And he has shown that today. He's committed to the club. He's committed to the fans. He knows how much people love him here.'

26 August 2000 – Vieira turns in a huge performance in a 5–3 victory over Charlton.

'When I heard the sanctions, I couldn't believe it. I feel like I have killed someone. I didn't even insult anybody. I just behaved as I think I had to.'

14 October 2000 – as Wenger receives a £100,000 fine and a twelve-match touchline ban imposed by the FA for 'holding' an official after the Sunderland game ...

'I will first appeal. If that doesn't work I may have to go to a legal court. I will consider it with a lawyer.'

... prompting a furious Wenger to get legal ...

'They listen to their officials and no one else. It's like when you go against the police.'

... suggesting that the FA investigation may have lacked something in impartiality.

'As long as I'm not behind bars.'

I February 2001 – on leaving his appeal hearing at the FA, when asked if he would be attending his usual Friday press conference.

'When you get a twelve-match ban and you have my clean disciplinary record, you have to look at why you got such a ban.'

2 February 2001 – at a Friday press conference, a free man, after his touchline ban is rescinded on appeal, and the £100,000 fine is reduced to £10,000 ...

'I feel I got a fair hearing and that I could defend my case well.'

... and Wenger seeks to draw a line under the ban episode ...

'Everybody in football has to respect the rules. I didn't fight the rules. I did fight the fact that I didn't commit the charge.'

... and get the final word on the matter.

'We will defend Patrick vigorously. I cannot accept the FA's stance.'

5 December 2000 – more trouble for Patrick Vieira as he faces a new three-match ban after the FA asks its 'video advisory panel' to review incidents involving him during Arsenal's televised Premiership game against Leeds. Once again, Wenger springs to his player's defence ...

'I am surprised that they [the FA] have said the referee saw neither incident as he was well positioned in each case.'

... pointing out that Vieira was not even booked during the game concerned.

DISCIPLINE 2

'You have to ask yourself if players are more likely to be punished if their matches are on TV. For me, it can only be right if everybody is put under the same scrutiny.'

10 February 2001 – after Vieira receives only a one-match ban on video evidence.

'There was a little bit of talking, but nothing physical. The game was physical, but all the rest was very nice afterwards!'

26 November 2000 – making light of events at Elland Road, where Dermot Gallagher had to be protected by stewards from angry Arsenal players after a game in which seven of them were booked.

'I saw Martin Keown defending himself with his elbow.'

5 May 2001 – Wenger clearly sees an incident involving his defender and Leeds striker Mark Viduka.

'I feel the three red cards we have had [this season] do not show any basic problem of attitude considering the fair play we have in the team.'

14 September 2001.

'You cannot win if you are only thinking of kicking people.'

13 October 2001.

'It's a bit the fashion to talk about Arsenal and their disciplinary record.'

28 December 2001 – Wenger fends off questions about Arsenal's on-field conduct, which are once again *á la mode* ...

'I'm often accused of being overprotective to my players but I won't change. I'll always stick up for them.'

... and sums up his attitude to the whole business.

'If I only get criticism of red cards and not dropped points, then I can take it.'

29 September 2001 – a statement of belief, after Martin Keown receives the 39th red card of the Wenger era.

DISCIPLINE 2

'I know you will laugh when I say I didn't see it.'

**30 October 2001 – variations on a theme of Wenger, after
Oleg Luzhny receives the 40th red card of the Wenger era.**

'Maybe we should try playing with ten men in training as
every game we seem to be in that situation.'

**23 December 2001 – festive humour, after Giovanni van
Bronckhorst receives the 43rd red card of the Wenger era.**

'When we have players sent off even if we think they are
wrong we accept it; we don't say a word – we just play on
and win the games.'

**31 January 2002 – after Luzhny receives Arsenal's eleventh red
card of the season at Blackburn. Arsenal won the game.**

'Everything is forbidden. To show emotion is forbidden. You have to create rules but for me spontaneous celebration is part of the game and I wouldn't want that to be cut out.'

10 September 2002 – reacting to the suggestion that Thierry Henry might be in trouble for revealing a T-shirt message after scoring against Manchester City. The T-shirt bore the words 'For the New Born Kyd', a reference to the new daughter of, er, Sharleen Spiteri, lead singer of Texas, and friend of the Arsenal striker. Henry's action was in breach of FA regulations, but on this occasion, no disciplinary action was taken against him. However, the FA did write to the Arsenal striker, to 'remind him' about appropriate T-shirt behaviour in the future.

'Perhaps Dennis had a nervous reaction.'

28 October 2002 – in response to the allegation that Dennis Bergkamp stamped on Blackburn's Nils-Eric Johansson, apparently unseen by the match referee.

DISCIPLINE 2

'If you believed in a conspiracy, you would become paranoid and the next step after that is schizophrenia, a feeling that the world is against you. I don't go in for that kind of momentum.'

8 November 2002 – a general comment on Arsenal's ongoing disciplinary problems ...

'When we go to the FA disciplinary hearings, we are used to coming back with a heavy bag.'

... with more specific comment to follow.

'Durkin is Durkin. What can we do about him?'

23 November 2002 – after referee Paul Durkin sends off Sol Campbell in a 3–2 defeat at Southampton. It is not the first time this referee has dismissed one of Arsène Wenger's players.

'I've not seen a replay of the incident but Martin [Keown] told me this morning that he's sorry.'

9 December 2002 – two days after another tempestuous game with Manchester United, in which Martin Keown pushed Ruud van Nistelrooy in the face. Keown was later fined £5,000 for his misconduct.

'Did Dennis elbow Bowyer? Yes. But did he mean to do it? I doubt it. It looked to me like he was protecting the ball and Bowyer ran into him.'

20 January 2003 – elbows again after a victory over West Ham is marred by an incident involving Dennis Bergkamp and Lee Bowyer.

'The red card was deserved.'

11 August 2003 – a new season, and perhaps a new attitude towards disciplinary matters, after Francis Jeffers receives the 50th red card of the Wenger era in the Community Shield game with Manchester United ...

'I frankly didn't see that.'

... or perhaps not, when asked about Sol Campbell apparently kicking out at a United player in the same game.

'No.'

21 September 2003 – and no, indeed, after another stormy game with Manchester United, in response to the question: 'Arsène, the television pictures suggest that at least two of your players pushed van Nistelrooy after the final whistle. Did you see that?' Unfortunately for Wenger, others did see the pictures concerned ...

'I think Van Nistelrooy does not help himself, frankly ... he looks like a nice boy but on the pitch it is not always fair behaviour.'

... of a game which involved another red card for Patrick Vieira after a clash with Manchester United's Ruud van Nistelrooy. After the incident, van Nistelrooy remained on the field, only to miss a last-minute penalty, prompting an aggressively mocking response from Arsenal's Martin Keown, and others.

'I have been in English football for seven years now and I have witnessed situations that were ten times worse that were not punished. That doesn't mean we were right but it does mean that some people get away here with some things they shouldn't get away with.'

26 September 2003 – the aftermath of the Old Trafford game continues …

'Some clubs can never be caught. It's like you say it's only for the Mercedes that the speed limit counts. Everyone else can drive as they want.'

… and continues …

'I have watched the video again and we overreacted on the penalty and after the final whistle, and I apologise for that. I'm sorry if we offended anyone and it will not happen again.'

… as Wenger offers an unqualified apology after Arsenal FC and six players were charged with misconduct for their deeds during the Battle of Old Trafford …

DISCIPLINE 2

'I don't say that what we did was right but people have reacted as though these players have killed somebody.'

... or perhaps not completely unqualified ...

'It's a Sky trial. There is one guy in a lorry who decides whether or not to show something again. It's not the FA.'

... as the media conspiracy theory rises up ...

'This is English football like it really is, not like when you speak on TV and everyone wants to be nicey-nice. It's how football really is here in England and, the way you [the media] react, it is like you have never seen anything like it. Frankly, it's laughable.'

... as a media-fuelled storm continues. At least in the media.

'I don't deny that, sometimes, we have excessive reactions which need to be kept in control.'

3 October 2003 – only now does Wenger have the chance for general reflection on the subject of player discipline.

Forty-niners

Events at the end of the Manchester United game on 21 September 2003 provoked a media frenzy that lasted for weeks, and Arsenal were eventually hit with a hefty fine and several suspensions for their disciplinary lapses at Old Trafford. But in the final analysis, it was the actual football played that day that had the greater significance.

When Ruud van Nistelrooy missed his last-minute penalty, it cost Manchester United the chance of victory over Arsenal in the Premiership. As events transpired, it would be the closest any team would get to doing so all season.

Astonishingly, the 2003–04 season saw Arsenal fulfil their manager's much-derided prophesy of 2002, and go through an entire Premiership season unbeaten. As this unprecedented achievement drew near in the spring of 2004, even the strictly one-game-at-a-time Arsène Wenger allowed himself to contemplate the size of his achievement.

But that was not the end of the story. The 2004–05 season began with Arsenal needing just three more games unbeaten to set a new record for the English top flight. With this achieved, Arsenal could then go on to extend their run towards the magical figure of fifty games without defeat.

'The fact that we were down to nearly eight men on the pitch and still won the game says a lot about the spirit of the team and how united it is.'

26 September 2003 – Arsenal beat Newcastle in the first game since the Battle of Old Trafford despite injuries to a number of players.

'We have played ten Premiership games of ninety minutes so far this season and for five seconds we didn't behave like we want to behave.'

31 October 2000 – still the Battle of Old Trafford saga trundles on, to the frustration of Wenger, who would prefer to mention that the ten games concerned involved no losses for Arsenal. Including a two-game run at the end of the previous season, Arsenal now sat on a 12-match unbeaten Premiership run.

'I am very proud of them.'

22 November 2003 – Arsenal's 3–0 win at Birmingham makes it thirteen games without defeat since the start of the season, a new Premiership record.

'I don't understand how an unbeaten run can be a problem, but everyone thinks differently.'

21 February 2004 – responding to suggestions that being undefeated somehow placed Arsenal under greater pressure than their rivals.

'We are in a good position, but I think this team is more than just about winning trophies. I respect a team that goes thirty games unbeaten in the League.'

28 March 2004 – so that'll be 32 in total, then.

'They have shown once again that when their backs are against the wall they can respond by playing fantastic football.'

9 April 2004 – after a Good Friday win over Liverpool ends an unholy week for Arsenal which saw them lose in the FA Cup and European Cup. But they were still unbeaten in the Premiership.

'We've been remarkably consistent, haven't lost a game and we have played stylish football. We have entertained people who just love football.'

25 April 2004 – after the still unbeaten Arsenal secure the Premiership at Spurs, with four games to spare.

'We have a good chance now.'

1 May 2004 – now 35 games without defeat in 2003–04 ...

'In fifty years' time ... people might still speak about it more than if you win the European Cup.'

... and an amazing achievement looms.

'There's no trophy for going through the season unbeaten, but it's history.'

9 May 2004 – after a win over Fulham leaves Arsenal one game away from an unbeaten season ...

'There's real history to be made and, certainly, football-wise, immortality.'

... the magnitude of which achievement is not lost on the team manager.

'As long as you believe, then it is possible. It's a fantastic moment. I always had that dream and to fulfil it is marvellous.'

15 May 2004 – minutes after the end of a Premiership season in which Arsenal's record was played 38, won 26, drawn 12, lost 0.

'You have every year a team who wins the Champions League, but you do not have every year a team who makes a record like this.'

16 May 2004 – during Arsenal's victory parade through the streets of Islington.

'What makes me happy is that everyone acknowledges that they have enjoyed watching us.'

18 May 2004 – enjoying the plaudits.

'We were on the ropes at 3–1 but our mental resources and physical quality helped us to bounce back.'

22 August 2004 – after Arsenal score four successive second-half goals against Middlesbrough, and equal Nottingham forest's record of 42 top-flight games unbeaten.

'I think it's something amazing.'

25 August 2004 – as Forest's old record is surpassed with a 3–0 win over Blackburn.

'This team reached some highs today.'

16 October 2004 – after victory over Aston Villa. This is Arsenal's 49th straight Premiership game without defeat, with the 50th game scheduled for Old Trafford on 24 October 2004.

Job

By the start of the 2004–05 season, Arsène Wenger had secured the status of a great manager within the history of English football. Despite ongoing problems of player discipline, Arsène Wenger the coach had created a team widely considered to be one of the most attractive ever to have played the game in England.

But in the 21st century, there is more to being a football manager than just the coaching of footballers. The modern manager must also be aware of the arts of business, of media presentation, of celebrity and of politics. The present-day manager has a responsibility not only to himself, but also to his players, his club, the supporters and the game of football at large, while all the time pursuing the apparently simple matter of winning football games.

By 2004, it was clear that Arsène Wenger was the master of a sometimes devilish job. So how has this studious Frenchman gone about defining the nature of his work? Once again, his own comments reveal much of his *modus operandi*.

'Instant success is demanded everywhere; it's the same all over the world. I believe you have to work with your ideas, do quality work, and after that hope for the best.'

22 September 1996 – at *that* press conference.

'For me, being a professional is not just playing once a week, and playing well from time to time: it's trying to be at your best every time.'

22 November 1996.

'Everybody was so happy and to keep them happy we need to win the championship again. That is why this job slowly drives you crazy.'

3 May 1998 – Arsenal win the Premiership to the delight of their supporters, and the team manager ponders the madness of it all.

'Every manager can only be successful if he gets his team to play the way that he holds deeply within himself ...'

'You're a manager because you love to win. That's the only thing that lets you survive ...'

'When you watch somebody driving a Formula One car round a Grand Prix track you ask yourself why he's not scared, how he can do it. But when you ask him, he'll tell you it's because he concentrates on what he has to do, thinks about the next curve. When you are a football manager, it's the same.'

16 May 1998 – in reflective mood before the FA Cup Final, as Wenger thinks of motor racing.

'We are facing a new problem, as there is a European fixture nearly every week and so rotation is an obligation.'

17 September 1999 – on the price of pursuing success at home and abroad.

'I don't want to go back to France to manage — ever.'

9 December 1999 – Wenger perhaps thinks back to his career at Monaco, when his team lost out regularly to a Marseille team who were subsequently revealed to have been involved in match-fixing.

'What is the pleasure of being an international manager? You never see the players and when you do have them you absolutely have to win.'

11 October 2000 – happy to work in the club environment.

'My job is not to show anger or frustration, but to arrive at a logical analysis of what happened and try to work out why. There is no normal reaction any more in football. When you lose, it is always too negative. When you win, too positive. I try to give small problems small importance and the right importance to the right problems.'

27 November 1998.

'Football is quite simple to analyse. The hard thing is to find the players who can do it.'

20 February 1999.

'When a player has fought for you for seven or eight years, it is so difficult to tell them they must now go, especially if they are playing well.'

13 September 1997 – thinking aloud on the subject of 33-year-old Ian Wright and one of the harder tasks of football management.

'The most important thing for a manager is the best interests of the club. It is impossible to keep all the players happy. If a player is happy being a substitute he is not doing his job properly.'

19 September 1997.

'Maybe today I have more pressure in my job than when I started, but now I have the feeling that I don't have to sacrifice anything because it has become my natural way to live.'

11 April 1999.

'It's important that we are involved in every competition, otherwise it is not easy to keep everybody happy.'

'Everybody has the same problems, but every team needs to have four strikers to have a good season.'

24 September 2000 – comments in response to concerns, after Dennis Bergkamp had hinted at his unhappiness at being just one forward in the Arsenal squad, alongside Thierry Henry, Sylvain Wiltord and Kanu.

'Once managers know they will be sacked after one or two bad results, they will not care about working at what makes the club strong.'

25 October 2001 – speaking up for the rights of managers after a spate of high-profile sackings.

'It is not my job to judge what people do. I am not a policeman.'

18 December 2001 – when asked what he thought of Thierry Henry's furious confrontation with referee Graham Poll after a home defeat by Newcastle. It was a game that prompted Newcastle manager Bobby Robson to say that Arsenal had 'forgotten how to lose'.

'From that game on, we didn't lose, so he was right.'

8 September 2002 – a chuffed Wenger recalls Robson's comment with Arsenal still unbeaten in 2002 ...

'If you want to last in this job you can't be a bad loser.'

... prompting more comment on the business of defeat.

'Sometimes, psychologically, you try to change things to break habits, but I'm not a witch doctor. I'm just a football coach.'

25 September 2002.

'Every week or, sometimes, three days, you have an exam, and you have to be successful and pass that exam.'

14 December 2003 – the studious Wenger reveals the continuous assessment of the modern football manager.

'You always have to try and convince people – fans, directors, players and press. You are always under scrutiny. It's an eternal gamble, an eternal game going on. You can only win respect by your behaviour, by doing your job well.'

11 January 2001 – and more on the details of the job.

'My job is to give people who work hard all week something to enjoy on Saturdays and Wednesdays.'

6 February 2004.

'When you are a player, you think, 'Me! Me! Me!' When you are a manager, you think 'You! You! You!'

8 February 2002.

'Who motivates the motivator?'

17 January 2005 – as Arsenal's title defence falters, another media war with Alex Ferguson continues, and Chelsea sit comfortably on top of the League, Arsène Wenger admits that his can be a lonely job at times.

Curios

One of the enduring features of Arsène Wenger's public statements has been their capacity to surprise the most seasoned of football followers. By no means has he been the first English club manager blessed with a ready turn of phrase, but few club bosses before Arsène Wenger have been so consistently able to make their comments leap out from the sports pages and into the mind of the discerning reader.

The finest of Wenger's comments are full of metaphor and allusion to fields of life removed from those of football. The weather, mathematics, religion and other sports have all inspired Wenger's utterances over the years. At their best, these soundbites exhibit a literary quality in their own right. But amongst Wenger's many comments are some with little in the way of cultural value.

On some rare occasions, the Arsenal manager's sentences have seemed to be devoid of meaning itself. But perhaps this is only to be expected, given the nature of Wenger's job. In the cliché-ridden world of English football, a world that produced a real individual to inspire the comic character of Ron Manager, Arsène Wenger, too, has lapsed into expressions of the banal, the boring and the plain bizarre.

'I am a thunderstorm protector.'

30 August 1997 – an intriguing choice of phrase to explain his readiness to defend Arsenal players from media criticism.

'I knew my players were ready. After a few years, you just know. It's like working for the weather forecast: you have a feeling whether it will rain or not.'

31 January 1999 – far from under the weather after a hard-fought 1–0 win over Chelsea.

'Sometimes you do something completely crazy; you don't think, you just do it … when you have a little doubt in your mind, doing something completely unexpected helps you. Just do it, don't think about it. That was important for him.'

1 October 2000 – and still a weather theme, after Thierry Henry's wonder goal against Manchester United ends the striker's six-game goal, ahem, drought.

'We could be playing snowball instead of football in Moscow.'

10 November 2000 – and Arsenal are drawn to play Spartak in the Russian capital.

'It will be cold, perhaps minus-20, but I have played before at minus-22 for Strasbourg in the UEFA Cup against Düsseldorf in 1980.'

19 November 2000 – revealing the depth of his meteorological memory in advance of the Moscow Champions League fixture.

'Conditions were the same for both sides and we cannot use that as an excuse.'

22 November 2000 – after Arsenal are frozen out 4–1 in Moscow.

'If [Ashley Cole] had said to me that he didn't feel he could play as he was in the middle of a thunderstorm, then, no, I wouldn't have picked him.'

31 January 2005 – a somewhat unsettled climate at Arsenal, as rumours of Chelsea's interest in Arsenal's left-back overshadow Wenger's preparations for a game with Manchester United.

'Ian [Wright] has a slight hamstring but [David] Platt has a big hamstring.'

20 January 1997 – Wenger updates the injury news from Highbury.

'When I was younger I was much more excited on the bench. But now I have some problems to get quickly up.'

10 January 1998 – already well versed in English smut?

'Maybe we should go to Lourdes before Sunday's game.'

3 April 1998 – two days before an FA Cup semi-final and both Ian Wright and Marc Overmars are struggling to be fit for the game. Frenchman Wenger ponders a trip to his homeland for a miracle cure.

'Gérard [Houllier] is an open-minded and passionate man. I am the opposite: stubborn and stupid. But sometimes stupid behaviour makes you win.'

27 November 1998 – discussing his fellow French manager at Liverpool.

'I must consider whether what looks very high in August is very high in November.'

11 December 1998 – on the subject of transfer fees, as it happens.

'I don't know how Mr Bean can stop me saying what I believe is right unless he puts me in jail.'

8 January 1999 – a comment that requires some explanation. On 28 December 1998, Patrick Vieira was sent off in a game with Charlton Athletic and Wenger publicly accused Charlton player Neil Redfearn of cheating to get Vieira dismissed. The remark prompted a censorious telephone call to Wenger from the newly appointed 'compliance officer' of the FA, who also happened to be an ex-police officer. His name was Graham Bean.

'If Ken Bates is thinking of suing me then he must be a very sensitive boy.'

May 1999 – after the then chairman of Chelsea had responded angrily to a Wenger suggestion that Bates's club were fuelling the Premiership wages boom.

CURIOS

'I'm just sorry West Ham lost a game because of my fault. Maybe I have to change my glasses.'

18 October 1999 – a sarcastic response to the then manager of West Ham United. Harry Redknapp had suggested that his player Paolo di Canio had been booked for diving during a defeat by Arsenal because Arsène Wenger had claimed publicly that Di Canio was prone to such behaviour. *'Moi?'* responds the Arsenal manager.

'Of the nine red cards this season, we probably deserved half of them.'

7 April 1999 – some curious arithmetic from Monsieur.

'We will just think of winning and not go out there with a computer.'

11 May 1999 – unconcerned with mathematical factors such as goal difference prior to the penultimate game of the season against Leeds United. Arsenal lost 1–0 – in binary.

'If Barcelona create ten chances and hit the bar five times then I will be happy with a draw.'

19 October 1999 – looking forward to a big European night at Wembley.

'You can have a fantastic European Cup but, if you finish fifteenth in the League, what does it mean? Next year you are nowhere.'

9 December 1999 – and perhaps addressing the question of priorities.

'In international competition sometimes not conceding a goal is one step better than scoring one.'

1 May 2000 – some curious logic, if not arithmetic.

'We measured last season at Manchester United that Thierry Henry made 84 sprints between ten and fifteen yards, with an average recovery time of 27.5 seconds over 90 minutes.'

19 September 2000 – Wenger hints at the science of football training at Arsenal.

'It was a 200 per cent certain penalty.'

17 October 1998 – after a game at Southampton in which the home side's Ken Monkou appeared to have fouled Arsenal's Nicolas Anelka in the penalty area. No penalty was awarded, let alone two.

'It was 100 per cent a sending-off.'

3 February 2004 – Wenger agrees wholly with the referee's decision to send off Martin Keown in a League Cup semi-final. That's all.

'If you tell me that tomorrow I fight Mike Tyson, but you give an advantage to Tyson, I say, "What's happening here?"'

21 April 2000 – and still annoyed about the perceived advantage gained by Manchester United by withdrawing from the 1999–2000 FA Cup.

'[Emmanuel] Petit is fit and, if I don't know today whether to play him, I will not know much tomorrow. Perhaps I just need another sleepless night.'

22 October 1999 – Wenger, for once, suggests uncertainty on a matter of team selection.

'I like [Robbie] Fowler. In fact, I love Fowler.'

22 December 2000 – passionate praise for the then-Liverpool striker.

'How can you build up a wall when the guy is just allowed to shoot? It was ridiculous to concede a goal like that. I don't think it should be accepted.'

21 August 2001 – after defeat by Leeds United which featured a goal from a quickly taken free-kick by Leeds' Ian Harte.

'It was a strange goal, I must concede that.'

18 January 2004 – after a victory at Aston Villa which featured a goal from a quickly taken free-kick by Arsenal's Thierry Henry ...

'I do not know what was said by the referee to Thierry. He took a quick decision. Fair or not, good or not, I do not know.'

... and Arsenal gain three points for sure.

'I don't really agree with the rule because it's difficult to defend.'

12 December 2004 – after another game, and another goal from a quickly taken free-kick by Arsenal's Thierry Henry, this time against Chelsea ...

'It's an intelligent exploitation of the rule.'

... and Wenger seems to have warmed to the idea.

'Maybe in future we will have three video interventions possible during the game that you can use tactically. Each team would have those three moments where they could say, "Stop, we challenge the decision of the referee and want the video panel to have a look at it."'

1 January 2002 – an apparently serious New Year proposal that teams be allowed 'joker' interventions against disputed refereeing decisions.

'The fact that I say we will win it does not mean we have won it.'

14 April 2002 – the word of Wenger on Arsenal's Premiership ambitions.

'A doctor does not go to an accident and ask a victim if he is a Manchester United or Arsenal fan before he treats him.'

10 September 2002 – somewhat riled after apparently serious complaints from other clubs that the England team were employing too many medical staff with Arsenal connections.

'Quite frankly, I expect a player to be dead after a game.'

13 September 2002 – in response to public protests of exhaustion by Arsenal's tireless superstar Patrick Vieira.

'There's something strange – it's not logical.'

16 September 2002 – a tale of two elbows. During the previous weekend's fixtures, both Arsenal's Thierry Henry and Manchester United's David Beckham were caught on camera using their elbows against opponents. Beckham's offence was witnessed by the match referee, and so the FA were powerless to take the matter further. But Henry did face an FA hearing, because his referee saw nothing.

'We try to be relaxed but not overconfident. I want my players to think that Sunderland might be as dangerous on their day as Real Madrid.'

6 October 2002 – after a home game against Sunderland, whose day it wasn't.

'The background looks like a lot of red cards.'

30 December 2002 – Wenger comments on Arsenal's revamped club badge.

'The fifth goal definitely killed the game.'

22 February 2003 – when Arsenal go 5–0 ahead at Manchester City in the 52nd minute, the game is over as a contest.

'When you say in French that you have no personality, it's not a compliment, but it's also not an insult.'

10 March 2003 – in response to another misconduct charge laid against Patrick Vieira, this time for allegedly calling referee Andy D'Urso 'a nobody with no personality'. Unimpressed with Wenger's argument, the FA gave Vieira a two-match ban.

'What is in the interest of Sol Campbell to do Solskjaer with an elbow?'

17 April 2003 – a little flustered after Sol Campbell's dismissal for striking a Manchester United player during a cauldron of a night at Highbury.

'There was no water underneath him but it was very nice.'

26 October 2003 – surely not suggesting that Charlton's Matt Holland 'dived' to earn his team a penalty and a 1–1 draw?

'I didn't even realise it was Christmas next week ... we will have a full training session on the 25th and in the afternoon we will travel to Birmingham – without a Christmas tree.'

21 December 2002 – Ebenezer Wenger outlines the festive season at Highbury.

'At 4–0 the game was over.'

24 August 2003 – another statement of the obvious after a stunning performance at Middlesbrough.

'We didn't think he would play on Sunday because he was suspended; that makes me think he has all the qualities to join Arsenal.'

3 February 2004 – in fine form after the purchase of José Antonio Reyes.

'Can you accept in the World Cup that Maradona scored with his hand? It's not the hand of God, if you have a video system and you will know straight away it's no goal.'

24 April 2004 – an argument for the use of video technology in football, as the French manager reveals once and for all that he knows those moments of football history felt most closely by English lovers of the game.

'We need to introduce video replays as quickly as possible.'

17 January 2005 – Wenger returns to the video argument, after a linesman's error denies Tottenham a clear last-minute winner in a game with Manchester United ...

'If you take the example of Manchester United, they would be in mid-table now if officials had the benefit of video replays.'

... with the suggestion that Ferguson's team had benefited from officiating errors more than once in the course of the 2004–05 season.

'You can sometimes miss ten chances and not score and only have one in the second half and score.'

2 April 2004.

'I was cool, but internally very happy. If I had started to jump around the pitch, you would have had to send me to a hospital! I was close to doing it though – and when I start, I can't stop!'

15 May 2004 – after Arsenal's final game of their unbeaten Premiership season, and their manager is, er, mad for it?

Big Business

In the aftermath of the 'Invincibles' season of 2003–04, Arsenal supporters might have anticipated a pleasant summer, basking in the unprecedented achievement of their team. Instead, they found themselves troubled by reports that their captain Patrick Vieira was ready to leave Arsenal for Spanish giants Real Madrid.

It was a story that ran for weeks, and even Arsène Wenger seemed unsure whether Vieira would stay or go. In the end, he stayed, to the delight of Arsenal fans, many of whom now saw Arsenal as a club big enough to see off the predatory activities of Real Madrid. If true, then this was a remarkable achievement in itself.

Throughout his time at Arsenal, Arsène Wenger has lived with the reality that there are bigger football clubs out there. In England, Wenger's Arsenal have always lagged behind Manchester United in terms of commercial might, and part of Wenger's achievement has been to compete on equal terms with United despite a relative financial disadvantage.

But even this disparity was eclipsed in 2003, when Russian billionaire Roman Abramovich took over Chelsea and set about spending his fortune on the team with astonishing speed. By the end of 2004, Arsenal were no more than the third-biggest club in England, but Wenger appeared to relish the new challenge posed by Abramovich's millions. It was not the first time he had to face up to the consequences of football as big business.

'I'm not a businessman, I'm a football manager, so what interests me is sport, and much less money.'

10 January 1998.

'It is not in my contract but if I thought Peter Hill-Wood, David Dein and Daniel Fiszman [Arsenal directors] would leave and that some media executive would come in and say, "Sell that player or buy that one", then, yes, it would be a worry. But I have total confidence in the people who employ me because I know they love the club so much and don't want to sell it.'

21 November 1998 – in response to rumours of a 'takeover' of Arsenal by the United News and Media Group.

'We live in a crazy world but not one where a player plays for his country when he has not yet returned for his club.'

13 February 2000 – refusing to release the injured Tony Adams for an England friendly match with Argentina.

BIG BUSINESS

'It's nonsense for Brazil to be playing in China in February.'

17 January 2003 – faced with the prospect of losing an Arsenal player [Gilberto Silva] for a meaningless international friendly, and not for the first or last time.

'I do not want to become a victim to the star system, when you go and buy a name but the player is dead.'

9 August 2000 – a comment on the whole business of big-money football transfers.

'If you don't have to balance the books you can imagine anything.'

13 August 2000 – referring to the seemingly bottomless coffers of some of Arsenal's European rivals.

'If players can move every three months, then it will not be football any more – but a circus.'

19 January 2001 – strong views on proposed EU reforms to football players' contracts which would give footballers the right to quit their clubs mid-contract.

'I'll give up club football if players can give three months' notice.'

11 February 2001 – very serious indeed as the contract debate continues.

'Can football survive by thinking the club is nothing any more except a railway station where players stay as long as they want and travel to somewhere else if they have to?'

23 February 2001 – Wenger maintains his high-profile opposition to contract reform, even appealing to Alex Ferguson for support.

'I just wanted to protect football, which is the game I love.'

7 March 2001 – after a compromise deal is reached between the EU and football's governing bodies, and Wenger talks down any threats to leave club football.

'Clubs cannot afford less income.'

10 September 2001 – a manager happy with the money-spinning second group-stage format then in place for the Champions League.

'We don't want to be the police of the Premier League. We don't want to be seen as a club who decides what is right and what is wrong. We just wanted to keep Patrick Vieira.'

17 August 2001 – Wenger seeks to close the subject of Manchester United's alleged impropriety in 'tapping up' Patrick Vieira.

'[Italian] clubs are stronger financially than the ones in England or Spain because they can sign individual contracts with the television companies. Italy is a very capitalistic country. It's extreme. Juventus have a big contract, but Chievo [and] Verona have nothing. If the big clubs in England could sign individual contracts with Sky, they would have very big incomes. Sky wouldn't be interested in buying the smaller clubs.'

27 November 2002 – on differences between England and Italy.

'To build a great team is not all about money. First you have to create spirit and togetherness in the squad and that's not easy.'

30 July 2003 – as the spending spree of the billionaire Chelsea owner Roman Abramovich continues with the £16 million purchase of Juan Sebastian Veron from Manchester United.

'Money doesn't give everything. But it helps.'

3 August 2003.

'Chelsea have won the Lottery and we cannot compete financially so we try to compete in a different way. What's important is what happens on the pitch.'

9 August 2003.

'How can you spend £100 million and say you are not a main challenger?'

2 September 2003 – as Abramovich's spending approaches a big milestone.

'We didn't spend much in the summer.'

1 September 2003 – in sharp contrast to the situation at Highbury.

219

BIG BUSINESS

'It's good that there's more money in the game, but it's just an isolated case in a very deflated football world ... Wages will be pushed up, but only [by] the players who are interesting Chelsea.'

12 September 2003.

'Chelsea have distorted the transfer market because they can buy any player, but it has been quiet for us because we don't have any money in comparison to them.'

30 July 2004 – as Abramovich's spending on players reaches £200 million in fourteen months.

'They [Chelsea] have bought great players – Drogba, Robben, Tiago, Carvalho, Ferreira, Cech. It makes a difference.'

15 January 2005 – as Chelsea go ten points clear at the top of the Premiership, money can't buy love, but it can buy footballers.

'If [Chelsea] want to buy [Ashley Cole] you should be capable of finding the phone number of Arsenal Football Club.'

31 January 2005 – Wenger responds to reports of clandestine meetings between his under-contract player and senior representatives of Chelsea.

'The most important thing is to be in the Champions League. It determines the way you run the club and the way the club survives.'

15 May 2001.

'If I want a player from Real Madrid, I would call Real Madrid first. I would not come out in the newspapers first.'

11 February 2004 – in response to rumours of illicit contact between Real Madrid and Thierry Henry.

'There is the worry that too much money has brought wealth to lots of people who do not care about football, only money. It's important to keep out these greedy people who hang around players and the game just because they can make more money.'

20 January 2001.

'I sometimes say to footballers' agents, "The difference between you and me is that, if tomorrow there were no more money in football, I'd still be here, but not you."'

N'est-ce pas?

'You can't just base a club on financial requirements as it does not work like that. Otherwise, you sell your best players and have a lot of money and no team!'

10 December 2003.

'I think that, always in a club, it's important that decisions have to be ruled by the fact that you want to be a better team, and not because you want to sell more shirts.'

24 February 2004 – commenting on the desire of many football executives to 'exploit' perceived commercial opportunities in the Far East.

'It's the usual summer story. It's newspaper talk.'

17 July 2004 – a confident response to the reports of contact between Vieira and Real Madrid ...

'Patrick's a big player for us but, if he wants to move on, then there's very little me or the club can do.'

... with an early admission that matters were not entirely in his own hands, in spite of Vieira's being contracted to Arsenal until 2007.

'I am not in Patrick's head. But I don't think he has an interest in Real Madrid.'

28 July 2004 – an apparently still confident Wenger admits his lack of telepathic skill.

'Why does Michael Schumacher stay at Ferrari? Because he knows he can win there.'

6 August 2004 – making the bold assertion that the Arsenal team could dominate European football in the way that the Ferrari team has dominated motor racing, and suggesting that Vieira's status as a footballer was akin to that of Schumacher as a racing driver ...

'I just think he's happy here. He's been a big part of the history of this team, and I want him to go to the end of what he can do here. To build a big club to the level where I want it to be takes ten years. I want him to go to the end of the vision I have for this team and this club.'

... with further praise for Vieira, past, present and future? ...

'Patrick is my mate but it's up to him what he does and we cannot affect him.'

... but still unsure of the intentions of *son ami*.

'Of course we want him to stay but if he wants to leave there would be an open door.'

8 August 2004 – a now-tetchy Wenger seeks to bring the saga to a conclusion, one way or another ...

224

'When he is clear in his head he has to come out and say what he wants to do, and he has to do that quickly, by Saturday.'

... setting Saturday, 14 August as the date by which Vieira's destiny must be decided.

'I am of course very pleased that Patrick is staying.'

13 August 2004 – an auspicious day for Arsenal's manager and their supporters ...

'It was one of the few occasions in our sport that money has played no part in a big story like this.'

... as Vieira finally decides to stay at Arsenal, quoting unbreakable love for the club as the reason, a decision of some historical import, at least according to Arsène Wenger.

'I am not a prophet.'

13 August 2004 – when asked how long the newly committed Patrick Vieira would remain at Arsenal. Some might disagree.

BIG BUSINESS

'They [Real Madrid] usually get what they want. This time it didn't work.'

3 September 2004 – an understandably pleased Arsenal manager reflects on the Vieira saga.

Familiar

And so the 2004–05 season began with Patrick Vieira still an Arsenal player, and Arsène Wenger poised to sign a third contract extension, keeping him at the club until 2008. The season kicked off with Wenger established as part of the furniture of English football, with his rivalry with Sir Alex Ferguson as fierce as ever, and with the advent of a new rival in Jose Mourinho at big-money Chelsea after winning the European Cup with Porto.

Predictably, Wenger was quick to address the new threat of Chelsea in his public comments but, in October 2004, it was the familiar rivalry with Manchester United that once again stoked the imagination and the indignation of the English media.

On this occasion, it was a first Premiership defeat for Arsenal in seventeen months that prompted a second 'Battle' to rank alongside the previous year's brouhaha at old Trafford. Afterwards, and once again, Wenger found himself addressing the question of player discipline, this time more off than on the field.

If nothing else, the aftermath of the Old Trafford defeat showed how deeply Wenger remained committed to Arsenal Football Club, and his contract extension meant that he would still be around when the club moved to its new 60,000-capacity stadium for the start of the 2006–07 season. And so it was with a familiar face on the touchline that Arsenal FC began their penultimate season at the Highbury stadium.

'Since I arrived at Arsenal in 1996, English football has changed in a huge manner ... it has changed for the better at every club. Training methods, the diet, the preparation, the professional organisation the training centres – everything is better.'

31 March 2001 – English football is used to the Wenger way.

'They [Arsenal FC] are very supportive. There was also a time when they had to be strong and they were.'

14 April 2004 – praise for the Arsenal directors who stuck by Wenger, most notably in the summer of 2001 when, after three seasons without a trophy, other boards might have ditched the manager.

'The confidence is there now. If it's not there now, it never will be.'

13 September 2004 – League champions, unbeaten since before the Flood, and Wenger is the most secure manager in English football.

'We are at the stage now where people expect a lot from us.'

29 September 2004.

'It is a sign of a good player to do something special when you don't expect it.'

15 February 2004 – on José Antonio Reyes's first goal for Arsenal – a 25-yard FA Cup scorcher against Chelsea. The young Spaniard then added a second to secure the game for Arsenal.

'This season is where it really starts for Reyes.'

7 August 2004 – prior to a new season with Reyes, just one of a number of youngsters new to the Arsenal first-team.

'Robin is a great young talent and a fantastic signing for the club.'

28 April 2004 – after signing Dutch striker Robin van Persie.

'[Francesc] Fabregas is only seventeen, but age is not important. We had a seventeen-year-old and a 35-year-old in Dennis Bergkamp and they both showed that age doesn't matter.'

15 August 2004 – the defence of the Premiership begins with Arsenal old and new combining to defeat Everton 4–1.

'I feel nothing major happened. It is not the first incident after a game and I hope it is not the last.'

1 October 2004 – commenting on an apparently serious disagreement on the Arsenal team coach after a Champions League tie in Norway. The argument was a heated affair involving Patrick Vieira and Lauren, and concerned apparent defensive failings by Arsenal in the course of the game. Far from concerned by an incident which eventually involved the Norwegian police, Wenger appeared to be encouraged ...

'It shows the players care ... professional matters matter to us.'

... before drawing a line under the whole affair.

'I want gladiators who are ready to go in with big commitment and with big passion.'

22 October 2004 – as the long-unbeaten Arsenal look forward to re-entering the Old Trafford arena.

'We got the usual penalty for Manchester United when they are in a difficult position. In a game like that, to see how lightly the referee gave a penalty is difficult to take.'

24 October 2004 – immediately after another stormy encounter with Manchester United involving a dubious penalty decision by referee Mike Riley. Arsenal's unbeaten run of games comes to an end at 49, and Wenger is furious, perhaps as never before ...

'We know how Ruud van Nistelrooy behaves. He can only cheat people who don't know him well.'

... not for the first time, Wenger deploys the C-word in describing the Manchester United striker Ruud van Nistelrooy, who escaped punishment for a serious foul on Arsenal's Ashley Cole, at least during the Old Trafford game.

'He [van Nistelrooy] always does it like he is innocent.
Play football, my friend, and forget about all the rest.'

**26 October 2004 – Wenger still fumes at United's Dutchman
who, unknown to Wenger at the time, was preparing to admit
his foul play against Ashley Cole and receive a three-match ban
as a consequence. But the fall-out from the Old Trafford game
was still far from over ...**

'I don't know what happened to Ferguson.'

**... as Wenger is asked about his own involvement in a post-
match tunnel incident in which the United manager was
allegedly pelted with pizza and soup by Arsenal players ...**

'I haven't seen it if šomething was thrown.'

... seemingly out of view of the Arsenal manager ...

'In the eight years I have been here I have lost against
some great Manchester United sides and I have just said,
"Listen, they are a fantastic football side." On Sunday, I
couldn't say that.'

**... who tries to shift the conversation back to the actual football
played at Old Trafford, or at least an interpretation of it.**

'We did a job today. Defeat would have put us in a confidence crisis. People would have said we could lose 49 on the trot.'

30 October 2004 – a second defeat in 51 games is only averted by a last-gasp equaliser by Robin van Persie against Southampton ...

'We are finished with it.'

... but Wenger is still forced back to the previous week's events at Old Trafford, now christened the 'Battle of the Buffet' by a delirious media.

'I don't see any need to have peace talks because we are not at war.'

12 November 2004 – now the media talks of some kind of summit meeting between Arsenal and Manchester United.

'At the moment we are not too concerned by Chelsea.'

28 November 2004 – Arsenal lose at Liverpool and Wenger is forced to address the potential of their table-topping London rivals. In his own way.

'Don't forget that last year [2003–04] Chelsea finished in front of Manchester United, so it's not a miracle they are fighting for the championship now.'

11 December 2004 – a showdown looms against moneybags Chelsea, whose manager Jose Mourinho was already showing a taste for the mind games so long the preserve of Arsène Wenger and Alex Ferguson.

'That's not the feeling I have.'

19 December 2004 – in response to Mourinho's own 'feeling' that his team were destined to win the 2004–05 Premiership.

'I didn't call him a cheat.'

16 December 2004 – Wenger defends his earlier comments about Ruud van Nistelrooy after he is charged with 'improper conduct' by the FA ...

'To have gone through everything that happened that day and for just me to be charged, you must have a good sense of humour.'

... prompting a pithy response from the Arsenal manager who would eventually receive a £15,000 fine for his comments after the Battle of the Buffet.

'Fewer fouls committed? Most sinned against? Who is it? Arsenal Football Club.'

31 January 2005 – as the rematch with United looms, Wenger points out that, for all Arsenal's reputation as a dirty team, their disciplinary record had actually become the best in the Premiership. Indeed, and without anybody noticing, Arsenal had now gone a year without a player being sent off ...

'I would say spontaneously that the losers are out of the title race.'

... but Wenger's priority is still results, as defeat for either Arsenal or United in the coming game would mean second best in the Premiership.

'It is Chelsea's title now. United still have a slight chance but there is too much for us to do. But we still have our pride and will keep trying as well as we can.'

I February 2005 – after Arsenal lose 4–2 to Manchester United at Highbury, and Wenger concedes the title to the new third force in the English domestic game, a Chelsea team whose miserly defence and habit of winning 1–0 reminded some viewers of an earlier age at Arsenal.

'We want to finish as close as possible to Chelsea. We think the future's bright.'

14 February 2005 – after Arsenal beat Crystal Palace 5–1 with a glorious exhibition of attacking football.

Revelation

In February 2005, Arsène Wenger was midway through his eighth full season as Arsenal manager, and many of his club's supporters looked forward to more successes in the future. To win Premierships and FA Cups, and to win them in style, was now part of the Arsenal way, and few supporters doubted the dominant role played by Arsène Wenger in this achievement.

Yet some Arsenal supporters yearned for greater glories still, and they could draw on the words of the team manager for support. On occasions, throughout his time at Highbury, Arsène Wenger has allowed himself to look ahead to the future. His 'unbeaten' prophesy of 2002 may be the most famous example of this, but numerous other public comments have made it clear that Wenger has a clear vision of Arsenal as an even greater club at an even greater home than Highbury.

Specifically, Wenger has talked time and again of a future where Arsenal fulfil their potential in European competition and, although his early experiences in Europe produced very little reward, there were few Arsenal supporters unconvinced that Arsène Wenger remained the man to take the club into the future for as long as he saw fit.

REVELATION

'You have to forget about what you have done in the past and look at what is in front of you.'

23 December 2001.

'Even when we were walking around the pitch in front of all those happy people, my first thought was about the European Champions League.'

16 May 1998 – looking back at lifting a first Premiership trophy, and looking forward beyond that afternoon's FA Cup Final.

'The future is very simple. We have to show that we can compete at the top level, to survive in the top three or four in the Premiership for a long period.'

8 December 1998.

'I see a move after my managerial career as a director or president of a club somewhere.'

... and Wenger looks far into the future of his career in football.

'It's a real regret to me that Arsenal have not yet played to their full potential in the Champions League. We need to establish the club as one of the top teams in that league. Historically, that's what the club is missing. You are not a great team until you have done that.'

27 October 1999.

'I believe that Arsenal can be one of the five biggest clubs in the world, because we have the basic support for it.'

21 April 2000.

'I want Arsenal to be the best club in the world.'

29 March 2001.

'I have a vision for this club. I want to help them move into a new stadium when this club can become one of the biggest clubs in the world.'

24 November 2001 – Arsenal's plans to move home continue to progress.

'I think there are 70,000–80,000 people ready to watch
Arsenal every week.'

5 December 2001.

'My ambition is for Arsenal to become the
best in Europe .'

**7 December 2001 – on signing a contract keeping him at
Arsenal until 2005.**

'I'm desperate to win the European Cup.'

21 December 2001.

'I just want to take the club as far as I can and like at
every big club it is a construction. There is a scaffolding
that you build up and up and up ... we want to become
the biggest club in the world ... if you look at the
potential of Arsenal with the new stadium, you cannot say
you want to be second best in the world.'

2 March 2002.

'The [stadium] project meant taking on a risk and [a] gamble, but it shows that we move on, get better and compete with the best. We never give up and we never accept defeat and fight to compete with the best.'

24 February 2004 – at a media event announcing the £357 million financial package secured to complete the still unnamed stadium at Ashburton Grove.

'One day, people will realise how well we've done. Every season we have been in the top two, and that's no small achievement because we haven't had more money than everybody else. Far from it.'

28 April 2002.

'Our challenge is to dominate English football.'

May 2002 – on ambitions in England.

'In terms of the record books, you have to recognise that Manchester United have achieved what we haven't – yet.'

26 February 2003.

'I would like to become so good we are disliked.'

20 September 2002.

'I've always said that if I have to leave one day I will go abroad. I will never leave Arsenal to go to another English team.'

2 October 2002.

'Why did I push the board to build our new stadium? It's all about keeping the players so that we can give them the same money as they could get somewhere else.'

4 October 2002 – looking forward to a future at Ashburton Grove.

'I would like to be remembered as the manager who won the European Cup for Arsenal for the first time.'

26 February 2003.

'As long as it is a disaster to come second, then it is not too bad.'

4 May 2003 – after once again finishing runners-up in the Premiership, Wenger reminds Arsenal fans that there are worse positions to be in.

'If the team goes well, you have the finances available. The players are linked with the vision we have for the stadium. It is part of becoming one of the biggest clubs in the world.'

10 December 2003.

'As long as you feel you can push the club higher, you want to be part of it.'

14 December 2003.

'I feel we can get better and better.'

12 May 2004.

'We will have money to spend on paying for the stadium and improving the team, whatever is more important at the time. It is nice to have the choice.'

5 October 2004 – at a press conference announcing that Arsenal's new home will be known as the Emirates Stadium, following the signing of a lucrative naming deal with the Dubai-based airline.

'I still have so much to achieve and my target is to drive this club on – not only by sustaining our recent success, but building upon it. These are exciting times for Arsenal and I'm proud to be the manager.'

28 October 2004.

'We are a young side now … I feel when you see the [Arsenal] players in training that the quality is there. But they are young. It's a fight against time.'

21 January 2005 – Wenger reflects on the arrival in the Arsenal first team of raw talents like Francesc Fabregas, Mathieu Flamini and Philippe Senderos.

'I still feel we can compete with Manchester United and Chelsea, but not financially. There is always a way to compete. It will just be in a different way. We have to bring in younger players and give them time to mature.'

6 February 2005 – explaining how a new generation of Arsenal players will meet the challenge of those big-money rivals.

'There is an age when you have to be strong enough to say, "that's it". I'm scared as well, because we all face that one day.'

1 October 2000 – a final word on the future.

Sources

In compiling the quotations contained within this book, I have sought to include only those statements made by Arsène Wenger in his public comments to the media. Typically, these comments have been made at press conferences prior to and after Arsenal matches, as well as at regular Friday media gatherings at Arsenal's training centre.

For the majority of the quotes, I have relied on online news sources, notably those of the *Daily Telegraph*, the *Guardian* and the BBC. I have also relied on the newspaper archive of Birmingham Central Library for some of the earlier quotations, which were reported originally in the *Times*, the *Independent* and the *Daily Mail*.

Since Arsène Wenger has made it his practice not to grant exclusive interviews with British journalists, it is the case that many of the quotations in this book can be found in a number of news sources, as well as in the books about the Arsenal manager that have been published in recent years.

I have relied on three of these books in my research, as follows:

The Professor by Myles Palmer, Third edition, Virgin Books, 2003.

Wenger – The Making of a Legend by Jasper Rees, Short Books, 2003.

The Glorious Game by Alex Fynn and Kevin Whitcher, Orion, 2003.